C000020063

Not I, but Christ

*The Christian's relationship with Jesus as typified
in the story of Saul and David*

by

Roy Hession

Rickfords Hill Publishing Ltd.

Published by

RICKFORDS HILL PUBLISHING LTD.

24 High Street, Winslow, Buckingham, MK18 3HF, UK.

www.rhpbooks.co.uk

Copyright © 1980 Roy Hession Book Trust

First Published in 1980
This edition 2015

Extracts from the Authorized Version of the Bible (the King James
Bible), the rights in which are vested in the Crown, are reproduced
by permission of the Crown's Patentee,
Cambridge University Press.

ISBN: 978–1–905044–43–6

Printed and bound in Great Britain
by CPI Group (UK) Ltd, Croydon CR0 4YY

Contents

I have been crucified with Christ: nevertheless I live; yet not I, but Christ liveth in me.

Galatians 2:20

First Thoughts

The story of the Bible can be regarded simply as the story of two men, Adam and Christ. Paul implies as much when he refers to Jesus Christ as 'the second man' in contrast to Adam, who is called 'the first man' (1 Corinthians 15:47). It is the story on the one hand of the sin of the first man and his failure to fulfil God's intentions, and on the other hand of the coming of the second Man to rescue the first from his miseries and take over from him. It tells of the bitter hostility of the first man for the Second, but of the love of the Second for the first and of the redemption which He has achieved on his behalf. And the story continues right up to the present, for Adam lives today as surely as Jesus Christ does.

The Old Testament is full of types and foreshadowings of Christ and of the gospel of which He is the centre, and nowhere in its pages is the story of the first man and the second Man so clearly typified as in the history of Israel's first two kings, Saul and David. It is the main purpose of this book to see in Saul a picture of Adam, that is ourselves, and in David a picture of Jesus Christ, and to see in the uneasy relationship between them a reflection of the state of things that too often exists between us and Jesus. We shall see in the undying love of David for Saul, notwithstanding all he had to suffer at his hands, a faint foreshadowing of the vast love of Christ for us His enemies;

and in the great magnanimity which David showed to
the remnants of the house of Saul when ultimately it was
broken in defeat (2 Samuel 9) we shall see a marvellous
portrayal of the grace of God towards us sons of Adam
when we too come to an end of ourselves.

   I am not concerned merely to show the beautiful parallels
between David and Christ, though that is a profitable exercise, but to see in it all a pictorial presentation of certain
great truths of the New Testament with regard to the
Christian life, notably of the words, 'not I, but Christ.'
These four great little words from Paul's letter to the
Galatians are perhaps the most complete description in the
New Testament of the heart of the Christian life and how
it is to be lived. The way in which they are illustrated in
the story of Saul and David can be seen the moment I say
that God's purpose in David, as he came back victorious
from slaying Goliath was not merely that he should have
saved Saul from defeat at the hands of the Philistines, but
that he should ultimately supplant him and rule instead.
Saul was glad enough for the salvation that David had
accomplished for him, but when he realized that David
was the one to supplant him and take over his throne,
he was not so glad. Indeed, he resisted it with might and
main right to the end, and the ultimate tragedy of his life
was attributable to that one fact.

   That is an illustration of the truth that Jesus has saved
our souls not merely to deliver us from judgement and
bring us to heaven, but to supplant us progressively as
king here and now. We are happy enough for Him to do
the former, but we are not so willing to let Him do the
latter, especially when it comes to practical issues in

relationships with others and so on. It is not the picture of a nation looking for a king, but rather of one king having to step down in favour of another King. But it is only as we are willing for just that on each point that He shows, that victory and revival come to our lives, for He alone is our victory.

I say no more just now; it is enough, I trust, for you to see the direction of these studies and to assure you they will not be merely academic or informative, but deeply personal and full of challenge and encouragement with regard to a practical walk with God in victory and fruitfulness.

Do not be deterred by the fact that you may not be familiar with many incidents in the story, which is a very full one. I will seek to take you by the hand and lead you through the whole fascinating history and we shall learn so much together on the way.

If you are unaccustomed to looking at the Old Testament as containing types of Christ and foreshadowings of the gospel, and should you wonder on what grounds we are entitled to look at David especially as a type of Christ, I have added an appendix in which the whole matter is discussed with the intention of removing queries and difficulties on these points. And inasmuch as the culminating final chapter introduces Solomon as a type of Christ in the glory of His millennial reign, a type necessary to give the complete picture of Jesus, I have added another appendix in order to give the rationale for looking at Solomon in this way. An enquiring mind might like to look at those two appendices first before getting into the book, in order to save himself being distracted from its main mes-

sage by queries which, I trust, are satisfactorily answered
in them.

Having said that, may I beg you not to look upon this
book in any sense as a treatise on typology, nor be occupied too much with the way in which the incidents of the
story are handled to illustrate Christian experience. You
could either be fascinated by this sort of exegesis, or be
taken aback by it. It is not the illustration that matters
either way so much as the truth illustrated. It is when this
old story is applied closely to ourselves and we begin to
see Jesus that we come to the part that we should really
'latch on to.' I have preached over this material for years,
and I know of no better or more complete illustration of
the whole revival message—but it is only an illustration.
'Sir, we would see Jesus' should, I suggest, be the attitude
of the reader. He is to be concerned with David only as he
points forward to Christ and with Saul only as he sees in
him a picture of himself.

The version of the Bible used throughout is the
Authorized Version, also called the King James Version.
Occasionally there are small emendations culled from the
Revised Version of 1885 (almost the same as the American
Standard Version of 1901), but I have not burdened the
reader by mentioning these.

                                        Roy Hession

Because thou hast rejected the word of the LORD, he hath also rejected thee from being king.

1 Samuel 15:23

1

The Rejected King

With what high hopes did the people of Israel accept Saul as their king when he was presented to them at Mizpeh! Samuel, too, shared those hopes, for when the lot was cast and confirmed the private anointing he had already performed on him, he said to all the people (1 Samuel 10:24), 'See ye him whom the Lord hath chosen.' Yes, even Samuel was caught up in the euphoria of that moment. True, he knew it had never been God's first purpose for them to have a king, since they already had one in Jehovah. He knew, too, that the people's request for a king was only because they had rejected the Lord from reigning over them. But, he reasoned, God had now assented to their request and had led in the most unmistakable way to this man and to his anointing of him. And now before all the people the lot had confirmed the anointing. First the tribe of Benjamin was taken, then the family of Matri, and finally of that family, Saul, the son of Kish. And, thought Samuel, was he not a man of becoming modesty, hiding among the stuff, when he should be receiving the acclaim of the people? Surely that boded well for the future. Above all, when he did appear, did he not look every inch a king, head and shoulders taller than any other? So it was that Samuel joyously said, 'See ye him whom the LORD hath chosen, that there is none like him among all the people!'

And yet only two years later, Samuel, as God's mouthpiece, is having to say to Saul, 'But now thy kingdom shall not continue; the LORD hath sought him a man after his own heart, and the LORD hath commanded him to be captain over his people.' That word referred to his dynasty; every king hoped that his sons would occupy the throne after him for many generations; but here the Lord says it was not going to happen; he had sought another man after His own heart for that. And then, two chapters later on, Samuel had to declare the Lord's rejection, not only of his dynasty, but of his personal rule right there and then. 'Because thou hast rejected the word of the LORD, he hath also rejected thee from being king.' So final was it that 'Samuel came no more to see Saul till the day of his death.' Though Saul was to continue to occupy the throne for years yet and attempted to function as ruler, he did so all the time as the rejected king.

If it be asked, why this summary rejection of his kingship, the answer is that almost from the beginning he began to violate the terms of his appointment. In acceding to the people's request for a king, God had not for one moment abrogated His own kingship. Saul was to be king only under God—just His vice-regent, so to speak. He was made king simply to do what God told him to do, to be His instrument of deliverance from the people's enemies and to mediate the divine rule to them. Thus, under authority to God in every detail, he would be clothed with authority. These were the terms of His appointment, and although not specifically stated in these words, they are clearly implied in every line of the story. But this was something

Saul could not, or would not understand. He did not see himself only as a king under orders to God, but as a king in his own right. He assumed that he was exalted to the throne to do what he liked, rather than what God told him. This was proved by the fact that whereas he would seem to obey, he always chose how far he would obey, just as far as pleased him. This trait came out in two important matters right at the beginning of his reign.

One of God's first purposes in appointing him is shown by His words to Samuel, 'Tomorrow about this time I will send thee a man out of the land of Benjamin, and thou shalt anoint him to be captain over my people Israel, *that he may save my people out of the hand of the Philistines*: for I have looked upon my people, because their cry is come unto me' (1 Samuel 9:16). Freedom was the people's most pressing need and it was for their freedom that Saul was appointed. But when Samuel anointed Saul, he told him clearly that before he struck the first blow against the Philistines, 'thou shalt go down before me to Gilgal: and, behold, I will come down unto thee, to offer burnt offerings and to sacrifice sacrifices of peace offerings; seven days shalt thou tarry till I come *and show thee what thou shalt do.*' This was God's enterprise and Saul must wait for God and His instructions. When at last the encounter was imminent he did indeed go to Gilgal, and he did indeed wait for Samuel and that for seven days, but not, it would seem, for the whole of the seventh day. Because the forces of the Philistines were building up while his own were melting away, and because Samuel had not yet arrived, he felt he could wait no longer, and, to use his own words, 'I forced myself therefore and offered a burnt offering.' It was indeed a dire situation in which he found himself, but it's very direness should have been the more reason to have waited on God and for God. Instead, he took things into his own hands and acted independently. And although his independent action expressed itself in a religious matter, the offering of a burnt offering, it was disobedience nonetheless. That incident was apparently enough to prove that Saul would only rule Israel according to his own haughty will, for when Samuel appeared, there followed the first word of censure: 'Thou hast done foolishly—thy kingdom shall not continue....' His action had shown that he was in basic violation of the terms of his appointment, that deep down he did not regard himself as a king under orders to God, but as a king in his own right. And to what further insubordination would such an attitude lead? This was the reason the sentence upon him was so summary and drastic.

Utterly destroy

The second incident took place later and was a further and more serious act of disobedience. He was here commanded, as God's vice-regent, to execute His justice on Israel's ancient oppressors, the corrupt Amalekites. They were all to be utterly destroyed—men, women and cattle. 'Spare them not' was the command. Here too he obeyed, but only partially. He possibly would not have obeyed at all had the commission to cut heads off not appealed to him; he was that sort of man! But he did it as his own will, rather than God's, as shown by the fact that here too he chose how far he would obey—till it suited him to do otherwise. He certainly destroyed the people with the edge of the sword; 'But Saul and the people spared Agag, and the best of the sheep, and of the oxen, and of the fatlings, and of the lambs, and all that was good, and would not utterly destroy them but everything that was vile and refuse, that they destroyed utterly' (1 Samuel 15:9). When confronted by Samuel, he excused his action once again on the ground of religion; it was 'to sacrifice unto the LORD thy God,' he said. But Samuel would have none of it and cried, 'Hath the LORD as great delight in burnt offerings and sacrifices, as in obeying the voice of the LORD? Behold, to obey is better than sacrifice, and to hearken than the fat of rams.' Then followed the final words of rejection, not merely of his dynasty, but of himself as the present King: 'Because thou hast rejected the word of the LORD, he hath also rejected thee from being king.' And when Saul, in pleading with Samuel, accidentally rent Samuel's mantle, the latter saw it as symbolic and said, 'The LORD hath rent the kingdom of Israel from thee this day, and hath given it to a neighbour of thine, that is better than thou.' And to emphasize that it was irrevocable he added, 'And also the Strength of Israel will not lie nor repent, for he is not a man, that he should repent.'

So it was clear that he was rejected from reigning over Israel because he first had rejected the word of the Lord and had violated the whole terms of his appointment. Thereafter he fills page after page of our Bibles as the rejected king, from whom the Spirit of the Lord has departed, vainly trying to be king nonetheless—a pathetic figure indeed, all the time to be replaced by a neighbour of his who is better than he. That neighbour, as the unfolding story reveals, is to be David, but as yet he has not appeared on the scene.

Man the rejected king

Saul in this aspect I take to be a picture of man, the rejected king, for such he is today. He had been appointed by God to be king over His earth, to rule it for Him. God told Adam to 'have dominion over the fish of the sea, and over the fowl of the air, and over the cattle, and over all the earth, and over every creeping thing that creepeth upon the earth' (Genesis 1:26). It would be interesting to speculate what that dominion involved, how great were the powers given to him. They clearly included power over creatures animate; did they also include dominion over things inanimate, such as the elements? The second Man certainly had power over them; did the first man have the same power before he fell? We can only speculate, but 'dominion' is a big word and can only mean that he was God's king, ruling everything on the earth, as far as it needed to be ruled.

But it was clear that the terms of his appointment were that he was to be only a king under God, having authority because he was under authority. The fact that God had imposed the one prohibition He did, that of not eating of the tree of the knowledge of good and evil, demonstrated the fact that Adam, king though he was, was accountable to a higher King. But just here Adam failed. In taking of the forbidden fruit, he demonstrated that he was assuming the position of a king in his own right, with freedom to do as he liked. It was that aspect of the temptation that attracted him most ('in the day ye eat thereof... *ye shall be as gods*') and accounted for him yielding to it. It was an act of insubordination to God whereby he violated, as Saul did, the whole terms of his appointment as king.

And the verdict on him as a result was in effect the same: 'Because thou has rejected the word of the LORD, he hath also rejected thee from being king.' Ceasing to be under authority to God, he lost the authority he once had. He who once ruled the beasts of the earth now fears them and has to protect himself against them; he who once had every fruit of the earth for the taking now has to battle with thistles and thorns and can only make the earth yield bread by the sweat of his brow; and he who once commanded the elements (if indeed that was part of his early powers) is helpless and fearful before them; and above all, he who once was destined to live as long as he chose (for he had unrestricted access to the tree of life) became subject to death, whether he chose or not. Behold man as God's rejected king! How are the mighty fallen! All his efforts since then have been to regain his lost powers over nature, but without success. Although he has certainly come a long way to make nature once again serve him, he will never finally make it. As long as men still have to die, man is the slave of nature, rather than its king. There are still remnants about him which show his past kingship, but 'the Lord has rent the kingdom' from him and given it to a neighbour of his, who is better than he.

A neighbour better than he

What's that, you ask—a neighbour of his who is better than he? Who is that? It is another Man, Jesus, the Man after God's own heart, the Son of God Who became Son of man and thus neighbour to the first man. To Him is given the kingship which the first man has been deprived of. This world, this universe, is yet to be ruled by a Man.

The first man proved a failure; the second Man will fulfil all God's will and prosper gloriously. It is interesting to note that according to the prophecies of Scripture He is always given the title 'the Son of man' in all the great events of the future which He will precipitate, such as His coming again, the putting down of His enemies and the establishing of His kingdom on earth. (See for example Daniel 7:13; Matthew 24:30.) Son of God He truly is, but He is going to act in these events in His capacity as the second Man, the last Adam.

Although this seems a gloomy message for the rejected king, it provides for him his one bit of hope, for it is given to him to enjoy all the benefits and blessings of the rule of the second Man, if he is prepared to bow to His kingship.

But will he? That is the question of all questions. You see, it is not like an electorate voting for the best president, or a nation choosing a good king and government to rule them. It is rather, as has already been said, one king stepping down in favour of another King—and that is a different matter. We shall see in coming pages that that was the struggle that Saul faced for years with regard to that neighbour of his who was destined to take his throne.

How does this apply?

Now the important thing is how all this applies to us individually, for apply it most certainly does. As sons of Adam we have all repeated his sin in the garden again and again. To begin with, each one of us has been anointed king over some territory or another which we are to rule for Him. What the territory is will vary from person to person. A husband and father has been anointed as head of the home that he may rule it for God so that the family may know the beneficence of the divine rule as communicated to them by its king. A wife and mother has also been given her own territory to rule. For some of us the territory over which we are anointed as king is some sphere of Christian service, the church led by its minister, the Bible class taught by its leader, or some other form of Christian service in which we have influence. In other cases the territory over which we are called to rule may be the sphere of secular employment, as the manager of a firm, the owner of a shop, the leader of a section in office or factory, or a teacher in a school. Whereas nearly all of us have those over us, we also often have those under us for whom we have responsibility. And if no other territory seems to be given us there is for each of us the territory of our own personality—a vast domain—and we are anointed to be king there, to rule and subdue it for God.

But we are made kings only under God, not kings in our own right. We are given that sphere, not to do in it what we like, but only what God commands, that others might get the blessing of it. Let those who know themselves kings in their spheres, recognize that they themselves have a King over them. That is what is meant by the divine title, 'the King of kings' (Revelation 19:16). How many kings there are about—well, Jehovah is the King of the whole lot of them. To none is accorded absolute power in his sphere; each is subservient and accountable to the One Who appointed him. Only as men are under authority do they have His authority and know His power.

However, it is just at this point that we, along with Saul and Adam, have failed. Their sin has been our sin. We have assumed that we are kings in our own right and have

acted and reacted accordingly, and others have suffered
at our hands as a result. This has happened both in our
families, among our friends, in our secular work and,
most culpable of all, in our Christian service and in the
work of our church. In assuming ourselves to be kings in
our own right, we have imposed our will on others, and
blazed forth in anger when we imagine our wishes have
been disregarded. We have acted for our own gratification
and advancement without scrupulous regard for the will
of God or the needs of others. As Lord Acton said, 'Power
tends to corrupt and absolute power corrupts absolutely.'
And we have assumed that in certain spheres at least we
have absolute power. But we have never been granted
that in any sphere at all, not even in the sphere of our
personalities. In all such spheres we are kings under orders
to God, and in acting in any other way we have violated,
as Saul did, the terms of our appointment.

We like Saul...

The actual details of Saul's violation may well
resemble closely the ways in which self-on-the-throne has
expressed itself in our own lives, though at first you might
fail to identify them. Saul's two violations, as we have
seen, were both cases of reserving for himself the right to
choose how far he would obey, and he excused them both
on the grounds of religious activity. First, we may need
to see that, like Saul, we have not waited for God in His
enterprises, as He commanded us to do—at least not fully.
The Bible tells us that He is a God Who 'worketh for him
that waiteth for him' (Isaiah 64:4). And we are to accept
in faith every moment of our waiting as a moment of His

working. But we have not waited on Him or for Him, but because He seemed to tarry we have 'forced ourselves' and acted independently of Him, taking action which He did not command, action which came out of the top of our head rather than from the depths of His heart. That is characteristic of the independent Saul within us.

Secondly, we may have spared something which God told us was to be utterly destroyed, just as Saul spared the best of the sheep. We have obeyed, but only partially. That which God has appointed to utter destruction are all expressions of the flesh, that is the self-centred ego. Every expression of that is to be judged and repented of, but we have thought that some such traits about us are not too bad, indeed that they can be useful in God's service, and we have spared them judgment. But God's purpose with regard to the works and expressions of the flesh is death, not dedication. Some of our natural gifts can indeed be used in God's service, but not before they have been freed from the clinging ivy of the flesh, not before self has relinquished its hold on them. But we have not relinquished that hold—with regard to some things, yes certainly, but with regard to other things, no. They are still functioning in the energy of the flesh and for its glory and not in the Holy Spirit. This partial obedience, this sparing of favoured sins, is also typical of the Saul in us.

As a result of all this, the same judgment is pronounced upon us as upon Saul; 'because thou hast rejected the word of the LORD, he hath also rejected thee from being king.' It is not that He rejects us as persons, for as believers we are accepted by Him forever in the Beloved, but He rejects us as being kings over that territory He has given us to rule. Because we have rejected the word of the Lord in so many points, and because of the mess we have made as a result, we are declared flops and failures, unfit to rule that territory. And He tells us He has rent it from us, and given it to a Neighbour of ours, Who is better than we. The Lord Jesus, that Neighbour Whom God has appointed, has not come merely to help us to be better Sauls. It is too late to improve Saul. The Saul within us has already shown himself to be what he is, and that his is the disposition that 'is not subject to the law of God, neither indeed can be' (Romans 8:7). Jesus has come to supplant us and take over from us, and that progressively in issue after issue. And He does so, not as someone exterior to ourselves, but in and through the personality of the failed saint himself. He comes to forgive us, of course, but of what avail a salvation which leaves self still a king in his own right? The mess he caused in the first place he will cause again—in perhaps more subtle and dangerous ways, if he is left in that position.

So it is that the progressive superseding by Christ of this Saul within us is the hard but prime necessity of the Christian life—hard, because we shall not like it any more than Saul did; prime, because in this way lies happiness and fruitfulness; anything less will mean failure and even disaster.

The message of the cross

These are not truths which depend only on the story of Saul and David, but rather truths which are plainly declared throughout the New Testament, of which these Old Testament incidents are simply illustrations. The declaration that man is rejected as king is the message of the cross of Jesus, and the anointing of Another as King instead of man is declared by God's raising of Jesus from the dead. The New Testament declares in Romans 8:3 that 'God, sending His own Son in the likeness of sinful flesh and as an offering for sin, condemned sin in the flesh.' He was not only bearing our sins, but wearing our likeness. He had already been made in the likeness of men (Philippians 2:8) at the manger; there was no question of humanity's sinfulness there. But at the cross something more terrible took place; He was made 'in the likeness of sinful flesh.' He became an effigy of the man who had caused all the trouble, or rather of that in man, the flesh, which had done so. And the moment He became that, God condemned Him, and He had to cry out, 'My God, my God, why hast thou forsaken me?' (Matthew 27:46). But God was not condemning the Son as the Son, but as the one whose likeness the Son was then wearing—me. In judging Jesus He in reality 'condemned sin in the flesh.' What a verdict that is upon man! What is it but the complete setting aside of him as king, that he might live again as God's humble, repentant subject, turning everything over to Jesus, raised from the dead. And if he should seek again to act or react as a king in his own right, he can look again to the cross and accept afresh that verdict on himself and be restored to that subject position.

That is exactly what the text at the head of our book, Galatians 2:20, teaches. 'I have been crucified with Christ,' that is, at the cross I have been judged in the judgment of Christ. When one pays another's debt, in the eyes of the law it is as if the debtor himself has paid it. Paul fastens on this and says, 'We thus judge, that one died for all, therefore all died' (2 Corinthians 5:14). The cross means

we were ended, not mended. The first man's history as
king was ended there, and God does not intend to mend
him, for He has raised One from the dead to take his place.
So it is that the text does not stop with us being crucified
with Christ, but goes on to say, 'nevertheless I live; yet
not I, but Christ liveth in me.' The kingdom has been rent
from the first man and given to the second Man, the Lord
from heaven, Who deigns to live in him and exercise His
rule over him and through him.

What should Saul have done?

Now what ideally should Saul have done when he
received this solemn verdict on himself? He should have
humbled himself and accepted it, saying something like,
'Having sinned as I have, I am rightly and properly rejected
from reigning over Israel, and as soon as this neighbour
comes along whom God has chosen and who is better than
I, I am prepared to step down and turn everything over to
him. It will be a privilege just to hold his hat!' But, you
say, that is more than can be expected of any man. That is
only because we are all Sauls. Though Saul actually did
say 'I have sinned' (he said it more than once), he would
not and could not get himself to accept God's verdict and
step down in favour of another. Although there were times
when he seemed to repent (on one occasion he confessed,
'I have played the fool and have erred exceedingly,' 1
Samuel 26:21), he was never willing for this basic step.
He insisted on struggling on as the rejected king and he
did so to inevitable disaster and tragedy. This is the story
that fills chapter after chapter in 1 Samuel, the story of the
man who would not be broken.

For our part, our response is to be the very one that Saul was not willing for; none else will do. We are to accept at ever deeper levels the divine verdict on ourselves that we are rejected kings, and we are to confess ourselves failures that He may take over in each situation and issue. This is not something we do only in an overall sense, giving mental assent to the truths of our identification with Christ in His death and resurrection. Nor is it only that in a moment of surrender we claim by faith that Galatians 2:20 be made true in our experience. It is all that, but much more practically, it is to be our response to the conviction of sin each time the Holy Spirit challenges us about something. It is not enough to confess, 'I have sinned,' but I must go right through to see that the particular sin in question shows that I am a failure, a Saul who acted as if he were king in his own right, and acknowledge that I am rightly and properly rejected from reigning in my sphere. This surely is something of what is meant by 'getting to the foot of the cross.' There, in that place, forgiveness of our sin and cleansing from all unrighteousness is assured through the blood of Jesus Christ—but more than that, He Himself moves into the place where I admit I am a failure and becomes in me that which I have been confessing I so woefully lack.

However, we do not always get through there as quickly as we should. I am reminded how years ago my wife and I were taking part in a missionary conference in North America. At one session a lady missionary gave a very honest testimony of how the Lord had dealt with her on the mission field over various things which had come in to mar her work and witness. My wife was to speak at the next session, and alluding to what we had just heard, began by saying, 'Praise the Lord for hearing a missionary confess herself a failure!' Immediately the missionary concerned became very disturbed in heart. She said to herself, 'Is that the impression I gave, that I am a failure? It is true that there were certain sins for which I needed forgiveness, but that surely does not mean that I am a failure.' And she lost her peace for two days and did not regain it until at last she confessed that that was what it did mean—she was a failure. It was an important turning point for her, for it gave Jesus a new opportunity with her. Sometimes in seeking to get right with God we too will confess certain things, but all the time telling ourselves and perhaps others that that was not really like us—just for a moment we acted out of character. But that is not the truth. We never acted so much in character, the character of Saul, as we did in that matter. And God expects us to confess that fact; only then is peace with God restored and does Jesus take over anew.

Mourning for Saul

Though Saul, as we have said, was never willing to accept himself as rejected from reigning over Israel, it seems, strangely, that Samuel had difficulties about it too. Although he was the one to pronounce the verdict on him, we read, 'Nevertheless Samuel mourned for Saul'— mourned for the fair promise of that life never to come to fruition, mourned for the dashing of his own high hopes of him and for the fact that his own anointing of him seemed to have gone wrong. It clouded Samuel's days and he went around heaving great sighs. So big a thing was this in Samuel that it was hindering God's purposes and the Lord had to say to him, 'How long wilt thou mourn for Saul, seeing I have rejected him from reigning over Israel? fill thine horn with oil and go... and anoint unto me him whom I name unto thee.' Instead of any further mourning he was to accept as final God's rejection of Saul and anoint the new king that God would show him.

Could it be that he had in effect not quite accepted the Lord's rejection of Saul and therefore was still mourning for him when he should be embarking on the new chapter under his successor? This much I know, that when I am not willing to accept myself as a sinner, I too mourn for Saul, 'the old man' as Paul calls him, mourning that I still find things in my heart that should not be there, mourning that I have not yet improved. I am mourning for self, instead of praising for Jesus and for His blood that makes all things new. And when I am thus mourning, it is because I am not gratefully accepting the judgment of myself as expressed in the cross of Jesus and not believing in the power of His blood to cleanse from the shame and regrets of sin. What an important word, then, is this. How often God has had to say to my soul, 'How long wilt thou mourn for Saul, seeing I have rejected him?'

There is really something rather comfortable in confessing ourselves as rejected kings. As John Bunyan said, 'He that is down need fear no fall.' It makes it easier for us to agree with God when He convicts us. It is no longer surprising to us when we are shown something of wrongful self in our lives—Saul, we know, is just like that. And then joyous, carefree faith in Jesus grows in the soil of such acknowledgement—I am a failure indeed, but He is my grand success and He is there to live His life again in me.

We will not sit down till he come hither.... And the Lord said, Arise, anoint him: for this is he.

1 Samuel 16:11–12

2

The Anointed King

Having seen how God set aside Saul, we now turn to the anointing of David, from the rejected king to the anointed king. Samuel certainly needed to turn from the one to the other. He had spent long enough mourning for Saul. The Lord's word to him now was, 'Fill thine horn with oil, and go, I will send thee to Jesse, the Bethlehemite: for I have provided me a king from among his sons' (1 Samuel 16:1).

That is very much a picture of the Christian who, disappointed with himself and his Christian experience, is looking for the answer that will bring him victory. If he is to accept himself as crucified and judged with Christ, and to cease to expect any good thing from Saul, that is from himself, where does he go from there? In recent years there has been a great seeking on the part of the Lord's people for the answer to the failure and emptiness of their Christian profession, and the lessons of the passage before us are relevant indeed.

First, notice the Lord's word, 'for I have provided me a king from among his sons.' The phrase 'provided me' in the Authorized Version is the courtly Elizabethan English for 'provided for myself .' This king is not to be provided for Israel so much as for the Lord. It was God who needed

a king; the first one failed Him; He needed one who really
would fulfil all His will, who really would rule for Him
and under Him. We must remember, therefore, that it is not
we who need the new king, it is God. We have failed Him,
we have not fulfilled all His will, but He has provided for
Himself just the One Who is the complete answer, even
if we, like Samuel at this point in the story, are yet to see
Who He is and how He can be all this.

So Samuel goes to the house of Jesse at Bethlehem, and
each of the sons of Jesse passes before him. First to come
is Eliab, as fine a specimen of manhood as you would ever
want to meet, and immediately Samuel says, 'Surely the
LORD's anointed is before Him.' But he was only judging
after the seeing of the eyes, as we often do, and the Lord
said to him, 'Look not on his countenance, or the height
of his stature, for I have refused him.' Son followed son,
seven of them, and of each Samuel had to say, 'Neither
hath the LORD chosen this.' It seemed his mission was to
yield no result.

The sons of Jesse

Let us stop for a moment at this point in the story
and consider what these seven sons of Jesse, each one
refused, might signify. I cannot, of course, claim them
to be authentic Scriptural types in the way that David
is a type of Christ (see Appendix 1), but I think we can
use them just as an illustration—and that of something
important. I want to regard them as picturing the various
things we have looked to and tried in order to achieve
the blessings of a more victorious life—things we must
do, attainments we must reach, rules we must keep,

certain spiritual experiences we must have, if the desire of our hearts is to be fulfilled. One teacher says one thing, another emphasizes another.

I hesitate to itemize in detail what these sons of Jesse might represent among Christians today, lest I miss the thing that is a son of Jesse to you personally, or lest I get you arguing with me as you defend some favoured formula or method for spiritual growth. Only God can show what is for us a son of Jesse, and when He does so, He invariably steals up on us on the side where we have no defences, and we capitulate. Suffice it to say that the sons of Jesse have this in common, that they are all subtle variants of the way of works; they all involve us in 'striving,' that is, trying to get the blessing we want, 'not by faith, but as it were by the works of the law' (Romans 9:32). It is invariably do, do, do. For this reason there is under the demands of the sons of Jesse no 'sitting down'—I allude to the verse at the head of this chapter. When you have done your best to meet these demands, your conscience tells you there is more you should have done to be blessed. Take the matter of your devotions as an illustration. You have grown slack, we will suppose, in your daily prayer and Bible reading.

'Daily?' you say; 'I never realized it ought to be daily,' and so you set a quarter of an hour aside each day for this.

Then you meet someone who tells you he always spends half an hour every day.

'Then I must spend half an hour every day,' you say to yourself; 'how else can I be blessed?'

Then you read a book which speaks of the necessity of the believer spending at least an hour a day. So you try

to stretch it to that, though frankly, you have a hard time
filling so long a period with prayer, but you struggle on.
Then to your horror, you meet someone who periodically
spends a whole night in prayer! At that you give up; you
just can't win; there is never any end to the demands of
the sons of Jesse, never any 'sitting down' as one who has
found what he is looking for.

Please understand that in speaking of our devotions I am
not picking on that particular form of activity as likely to
be specially a son of Jesse. Your son of Jesse may well be
quite other, something which only God can show. I have
mentioned this one purely as an illustration that what the
sons of Jesse represent is not grace, but invariably some
form of law, something on the doing of which greater
blessing depends. They all ask us to come as something
other than empty sinners, and for that reason they do not
provide the answer. Jim Elliott, the young missionary who
lost his life bringing the gospel to the Auca Indians, said
a very profound thing for so young a man—'If it isn't
of grace, it isn't of God.' If you are a preacher, I know
you do not intend to teach law rather than grace, but be
assured, that is the way it can come over to your hearers.
Of course, you may not be a preacher at all—and yet I
think you are. All of us are; we preach to our own hearts,
if to no other. And so often the message we preach is one
that only sets us 'striving' in our own strength and that
ultimately leads us to despair because we cannot attain.
'The commandment, which was ordained to life'—if
I could keep it—'I found to be unto death'—because I
didn't, and it therefore only condemned me. So said Paul
in Romans 7:10. On the other hand, if you do manage to
keep it, or imagine you do, it will probably lead you to

pride when you compare yourself with others. Indeed, this
is one of the ways you can identify the sons of Jesse—by
the results, leading you either to despair on the one hand,
or pride on the other.

Arise, anoint him

Samuel, having failed to find his man among the seven
sons, asked Jesse, 'Are here all thy children?' Jesse
replied, 'There remaineth yet the youngest, and, behold,
he keepeth the sheep.' He had hardly thought it worth
calling so young and insignificant a lad.

Then Samuel said, getting excited, 'Send and fetch
him *for we will not sit down till he come hither.*' That last
sentence is a great gospel text, and we shall look at it more
closely in a moment.

When David was at last brought in, what a picture he
presents to us of our Lord Jesus. 'Now he was ruddy, and
withal of a beautiful countenance, and goodly to look
upon. And the LORD said, Arise, anoint him: for this is he.'
And Samuel did so, knowing he had found his man, or
rather God's man.

The words in which David's appearance was described
remind us of the way in which the maiden described her
Solomon in the book that bears his name: 'My beloved is
white and ruddy, the chiefest among ten thousand... his
mouth is most sweet; yea, he is altogether lovely. This
is my beloved, and this is my friend, O daughters of
Jerusalem' (Song of Solomon 5:10, 16). And those words
have, in turn, always been a favoured way in which the
saints and their hymn writers have described their Jesus...
altogether lovely, the chiefest among ten thousand.

We see portrayed in David, then, the attractiveness of the Lord Jesus, and it is an attractiveness that appeals, strangely, to sinners, as shown by the fact those who have been drawn to Him are all such. The word 'chiefest' in the phrase 'chiefest among ten thousand' means literally in the Hebrew, distinguished, that is, He excels all others in His charm. Psalm 45, without doubt truly messianic, says the same of Him (verse 2): 'Thou art fairer than the children of men.' Now, wherein is He fairer than all the sons of men? The next phrase in the psalm gives us the answer: 'grace is poured into thy lips.' It is the quality of grace which marks Him out as fairer than all others and grace is His attitude to sinners. How hard and censorious sinners are to their fellow sinners! Not so the Lord Jesus. Grace is not only poured into His lips; it also pours forth from His lips. Luke says in his account, 'All... wondered at the gracious words [i.e. words of grace] which proceeded out of His mouth' (Luke 4:22).

Grace is not only love, it is undeserved love. God loves all that He has made, but when the object of that love is utterly undeserving, wrong and wretched, and when that love does not change because of this, but proceeds to act on behalf of the undeserving one, then that love is called by another name—grace. This is the quality in the divine character which is the brightest gem in the crown God wears. This is the attribute He delights to demonstrate more than any other. And Jesus is the embodiment of that grace. As the apostle John says, 'The law was given by Moses; grace and truth came by Jesus Christ' (John 1:17). Instead of blaming sinners, Jesus has died for them and has in this way taken the blame out of sin. So a man's sins and failures need not cut him off, for, if honestly confessed, they become his one qualification for the grace that is greater than all his sin. This is what attracts sinners to Him. This is what makes Him 'fairer than all the sons of men.' To treat sinners as He does is not after the manner of men and therefore He excels them all.

We can sit down

We must now proceed to apply the words, 'We will not sit down till he comes hither.' We have seen that under the law and its subtle variants, there is no 'sitting down.' Not so with Him. When He comes, we do indeed sit down, that is, rest from our own works as a means to blessing, for we find in Him, as a gift, the satisfaction we had sought by those works. And we can sit down because He has first sat down. You see, there is only one thing wrong with the whole lot of us, saint and sinner alike, and that is sin; and He so fully put that away by the sacrifice of Himself that He could sit down. 'When he had by Himself purged our sins, [he] sat down...' (Hebrews 1:3). 'This man, after he had offered one sacrifice for sins forever, sat down...' (Hebrews 10:12). There is nothing more He needs to do to put the sinner or the failing saint utterly right with God. And when He comes, He invites us, who like the priests of old have been 'standing daily ministering and offering oftentimes the same sacrifices, which can never take away sins' (Hebrews 10:11) to sit down with Him and share His rest. 'He that is entered into his rest, he also hath ceased from his own works, as God did from his' in creation (Hebrews 4:10), and as Jesus did from His in redemption.

But a living experience of this is only when He 'comes hither.' It is only as He comes afresh to me in my need and I have revealed to me by the Spirit the meaning of His blood, that is, His finished work on the cross, that I can sit down.

However, in our sitting down there needs to be repentance of that which has brought us into our needy situation. The alternative is not between struggling and resting; there is something which must come between the two. In various matters we may have departed from the Lord in those subtle ways that any Christian can. There must be a returning, a repenting there, before we can sit down and rest in the value of His blood. But having repented, we not only can, but must rest in that work of His, if we are to find peace. This is the message of Isaiah 30:15, 'In returning and rest shall ye be saved'—not, mark you, in returning and resolving (that would only put us back under the law, depending on our own strength), but in returning and resting.

The end of the struggle

Then what a significance there is in the words, 'Arise, anoint him: for this is he'—especially the phrase, 'this is he.' This is always the work of the Holy Spirit to every seeker after the answer. When all else he has tried fails him, the Spirit points him to Jesus and says 'This is He.' As Phillips' paraphrase of Romans 10:4 says, 'Christ means the end of the struggle for righteousness-by-the-law for everyone who believes in him.' How we have struggled for righteousness (that is, to be right with God) and for peace, for power, for revival! But at last Jesus 'comes hither,' and that is the end of the struggle, for He is Himself the blessing that we seek and the easily accessible way to that blessing, available to us as we are and where we are. This may not immediately mean revival in the wide sense commonly understood by that word, but it certainly is revival for the one who finds Him anew, and revival has certainly got to begin somewhere; why not in him?

The balance of truth

Let me pause here to bring in another aspect of truth to balance what has been said. A one-sided presentation can create more problems than it solves, but in the Bible truth is always finely balanced.

I am thinking at this point of what I have said about the possibility of our devotions being 'sons of Jesse' to us, a form of legalism to which we may get into bondage and which might drive us to despair. As I have said, this is only an illustration of the various 'sons of Jesse', but having mentioned it I must correct a possible misapprehension.

It might be thought that once we have found Christ as the end of the struggle for peace and fullness, private prayer and study of the word of God will not be a special occupation with us. Actually, the opposite is the truth. Finding Christ as the end of our struggle will lead us to want to spend more time in these holy exercises rather than less. But there will be this difference; they are no longer objects of trust to us as they were before, things that we were doing self-consciously, hoping thereby to advance ourselves in holiness. We are finding what we need in Jesus Himself, Who is available to us as readily in our weakest moments as in our strongest. Finding Him so, we feel ourselves possessed with a new appetite and longing for prayer, worship and His word. If we have any complaint, it is that sometimes various earthly duties cause us to cut short those times with the Lord in which we were finding such delight. Such times, of course, give us even clearer views of Christ, which in turn stimulate us yet more, until we feel we could be praying and praising for ever—but the needs of others call us. And we respond to those needs and other affairs with the light of glory on our faces and in our hearts. This is a far cry from the all too common legal view of devotions, which yield no such blessing because we are looking directly to them rather than to Jesus alone. So it is we find that Christ is the way to our devotions, rather than they the way to Him; they are not the cause, but rather the consequence of His life in our hearts.

If, however, we have not such an appetite for, and enjoyment of private prayer and the word, then it is a symptom that something has gone wrong in our relationship with the Lord Jesus. The answer in such a case is not to try to make new promises with regard to our devotions, but rather to repent of what has gone wrong and get right with Him. Then Jesus becomes again the way to the enjoyment of prayer, praise and the word, and He will lead us to the form and time of them which is appropriate to our situation.

Beginning at the end

To return to our picture of the anointing of David there are two further things I need to mention. The finding and anointing of David was not the end, but the beginning. From that moment there began God's process of David displacing Saul so that he might be the new king. Much had to happen; there was resistance on Saul's part and

long patience on David's, but in the end it took place as
God said it would.

So it is with us. Finding Jesus as the end of the struggle
is not the end of the story as it might seem to us, but rather
the beginning. Now can begin the process whereby Jesus
progressively supplants me as king, as I 'break' before
Him. There will be many convictions of sin, but if I have
accepted that I am the rejected king and Jesus my all-
sufficient Anointed King, there will be a new readiness to
say yes to Him each time, and each time He will be King
in my place.

Then, whereas the Spirit of the Lord came on David,
the same Spirit departed from Saul, and he seemed to be
worse rather than better. And we too may feel that since
we entered into these things, we have not improved at all,
but rather the reverse. Day by day we seem to have more
to repent rather than less. Actually, we are not getting any
worse; Saul is as bad as he has ever been. The light is
simply shining more brightly and we have become more
sensitive and more obedient. The reward of light obeyed
is more light, by which we see more. Beware that in the
process you do not go back to mourning for Saul, instead
of praising for the blood of Jesus, which so fully cleanses
what is being revealed.

> O may the least omission pain
> My well-instructed soul,
> And drive me to the blood again
> That makes the wounded whole.

And who wrote those words? Charles Wesley, who
else?

So David prevailed over the Philistine with a sling and with a stone.

1 Samuel 17:50

3

The Anointed King and Goliath

Our story now becomes fascinating to say the least. We have come to the point where there are two kings in the nation. On the one hand there is Saul, the rejected king, unwilling to accept the fact and still trying to carry on. On the other hand there is David, the anointed king, though quite unknown as such to the people and to Saul. After the quiet, unpublicized anointing in the midst of his brethren, David was content to go back to keeping his father's sheep and remained in obscurity. True, he was called upon to play his harp before Saul to calm him in his dark depressions, and Saul loved him and made him his armour-bearer. But that was no permanent position. It seems he continued to keep the sheep, going to and fro between the court and his home to do so. Indeed, when later David went against Goliath, Saul did not even know who he was, and had to ask Abner, 'Whose son is this?' And Abner did not know either. Certainly this new God-given status was quite unrecognized and he himself did nothing to further it.

When God's time for him to appear did come, the first act of this youth, God's anointed king, was to undertake a task which Saul had been powerless to do, and by that one act to save Israel from servitude to the Philistines.

Nowhere was the failure of Saul more apparent than in his inability to take up the challenge of Goliath, and nowhere was the superiority of David more clearly seen than in his bringing down the giant, and that with nothing more than a sling and a stone.

Here is pictured the great victory which the second Man has wrought on behalf of the first man. Nowhere is the latter's failure more clearly seen than in his inability to find an answer to the challenge of sin and Satan. He may appear to have made many advances, as in the realm of technology, but when it comes to the moral sphere and to the accusations of Satan with regard to his falling short there, he is as bankrupt as he ever was. This is failure indeed, because herein lies the source of his other miseries. But it is exactly in this sphere that Jesus Christ excels. Alone He has triumphed gloriously over the foe that was too strong for man. And He knows how to implement that triumph in human lives.

Give me a man

Let us look first of all at Goliath. He must have been a frightening sight to the Israelites—eleven and a half feet tall, with armour all over him to match—and a huge, deadly javelin. The dimensions and weight of it all are given in the narrative. Only a man of Goliath's height and strength could have carried such armament and weaponry, let alone use them to effect. But Goliath could certainly do both!

What particularly terrified the Israelites was the nature of the challenge he gave. In olden times it was sometimes agreed that the issue of the battle would be decided not by the two armies fighting it out, but by single combat between two champions, one from either side, and the nation represented by the one slain would become the servants of the other. This is what Goliath proposed.

'Why are ye come out to set your battle in array?' he shouted. 'Am not I a Philistine, and ye servants of Saul? choose you a man for you, and let him come down to me. If he be able to fight with me, and to kill me, then will we be your servants: but if I prevail against him, and kill him, then shall ye be our servants, and serve us' (1 Samuel 17:8–9).

But whom would they choose? The obvious one to respond to Goliath's challenge should have been Saul, so much taller than any other Israelite. But he knew himself to be the rejected king; God had departed from him, and he did not dare. Neither did anybody else. And so it was that Goliath's challenge remained unanswered. His words, 'Give me a man, that we may fight together,' echoed round the valley of Elah on opposite sides of which the armies were drawn up, and that continued day after day, morning and evening, for forty days. It was always the same, 'Give me a man, Give me a man!' But there was no man, and for lack of a champion Israel faced certain servitude to the Philistines. What a situation! And it was into this situation that the young David came, when he visited his brothers who were serving in Saul's army.

The dominion of Satan

Now this is a picture of man under the power of Satan. Just as Israel, for lack of a champion, was dominated by Goliath, so are men under the dominion of Satan. That is how the New Testament describes man's condition. In one place it is said, 'the whole world lieth in the evil one' (1 John 5:19). In another place Paul defines his commission as being to turn men 'from the power of Satan unto God' (Acts 26:18) by the gospel. Jesus called Satan 'the prince of this world' (John 12:31) and Paul spoke of him as 'the god of this world' (2 Corinthians 4:4).

Now let me explain what it is that gives the devil his dominion over men, and in what that dominion consists. That which has given him power over men is sin. It is a law of the universe that the wages of sin is death. Of course it is the Bible that says this (Romans 6:23) but the Bible is only expressing a principle built into the nature of things that to break the moral law, on which all human life is built, always brings death in one form or another, whether we like it or not. So this edict is both implied in the law of the universe and declared specifically by the law of God. And it is the fact that all have sinned which brings men under the power of Satan. It might not be too fanciful to regard him as being in the position of a jailor who keeps in prison those who have broken the law of the land, pending their execution. He holds those whom the law of God has condemned and sees to it that they get the death due to sin in good measure here and now, even before they endure physical death and the subsequent 'second death,' which is eternal separation from God. Not even God can challenge this right, since it is based on His own laws; rather He concedes it, for He speaks of the devil as 'he who has the power of death, that is, the devil' (Hebrews 2:14).

In practice, the devil's power over us works out on the

level of accusation. He points to a man's weaknesses, and asks, 'How can you call yourself a Christian—you are not good enough?' And the man in question goes around with a bad conscience, never feeling adequate or worthy enough. If he engages in spiritual exercises and Christian activities, a little demon, so to speak, sits on his shoulder whispering in his ear, 'hypocrite, hypocrite!' and the man in question falters and his hands hang down. This in turn leads him to further sin; he feels so cut off from God that a bit more sin is not going to make much difference anyway, and so he indulges the more, only to be the more condemned.

This is the basic reason why the devil gets a man to sin at all—not merely to get him to do something unethical, but in order to give himself the ground on which then to accuse him and thus have, like a blackmailer, a hold over him.

Sometimes this leads a man not only to further sin, but to go back from the Lord altogether. He has heard the word 'hypocrite' in his ears so often that he has decided he will be such no longer and he gives up all profession of being a Christian. Now if he does not act like one, he cannot be accused of being a hypocrite. This is the rationale behind some seemingly inexplicable cases of apostasy.

All the later effects of sin, then, are based on this basic power of Satan over us, the power to accuse us, for which accusations we have no answer. Satan, however, is all the time challenging us to find one by, for instance, making ourselves the better men who can stand up to him and whom he cannot accuse. And we try to do so—we make a fuller consecration of ourselves to God, we espouse higher standards, we make many promises—only to fail again.

And the very standards we embraced and the promises we made only give Satan more to accuse us of, and we fall under his dominion even further. We have limitless power to commit sin, but once it is committed, we have no power at all to atone for it, or to extricate ourselves from the complications it so often brings. We are not only guilty sinners, nor only rebellious sinners, but especially are we *helpless* sinners, sinners 'without strength,' as Paul put it (Romans 5:6). We have got ourselves into our situation and nothing we can do will get us out of it. 'Give me a man,' said Goliath to Israel. 'Give me a man,' says Satan to us, 'be thou the man that can stand up to me.' And we know we are not that man, and for lack of a champion it seems we must face this servitude forever.

You might not express your experience of Goliath in exactly the way I have. You would perhaps talk of your despair, unhappiness, inadequacy, depression, lack of peace, difficult relationships with others; but you can be sure that these are the truths that lie behind it all and explain it.

God's champion

This, then, was Israel's plight, and it is ours. And it touched God's heart. If the appointing of Saul as king in the first place was because, to quote, 'I have looked upon My people, because their cry is come unto me' (1 Samuel 9:16), we can be sure that cry was still coming up to Him, all the more because that first king had failed them. And God had His champion in reserve against this very day— the shepherd boy, David. Though Goliath utterly dwarfed him, God was with him, and that was enough. And what a glorious victory he achieved, not only for himself, but for Israel. He became quite literally the saviour of Saul and his people that day.

It was the same with Jesus. Although for long centuries Satan thought there was none to answer his 'Give me a man,' God had His champion in reserve. He had Him there before ever sin brought man under the dominion of Satan, so that, as soon as the first sin was committed, God spoke of Him as the seed of the woman who would bruise the serpent's head. And in due time, right into the midst of man's despair and misery, He came.

> O loving wisdom of our God!
> When all was sin and shame,
> A second Adam to the fight,
> And to the rescue came.

He went alone

I do not repeat here the details of the breathless story of David's daring exploit, but rather bring out matters in which he is a type of Christ.

Notice first, he went alone. Because none else would go, he went. Strong men, who should have gone but did not dare, watched that lone figure, shamed and fascinated.

So of Jesus. We had no power to deliver ourselves; if we were to be saved, He would have to do it all—and that alone. None shared His sorrows, not even with their sympathy. He said to His disciples in Gethsemane, 'What, could ye not watch with me one hour?' In any case, no man could share the task itself with Him. What had to be done was possible only to the Son of God.

He went in weakness

Then David went in weakness. He deliberately laid aside Saul's proffered armour and went with nothing more than a sling, five smooth stones and faith in the Lord of hosts. It was the very opposite of what all men of war would have thought reasonable.

And that is how the Son of man went against our mighty foe—in weakness. He chose it that way. He denied Himself all earthly help: 'Put up thy sword into the sheath,' He said to Peter; 'the cup which my Father hath given me, shall I not drink it?' (John 18:11). He also denied Himself any heavenly help: 'Thinkest thou not that I cannot now pray to my Father, and he shall even now send me more than twelve legions of angels?' In another place He said, 'This is your hour, and the power of darkness' (Luke 22:53) and He submitted without struggle to what the devil had determined to do. The well-known text, 'He loved me, and gave himself for me' (Galatians 2:20) is literally in the Greek, '...and gave himself up for me.' That is just what He did—He gave Himself up to Satan's emissaries as they came to arrest Him. His strategy was not to meet might with might, but with weakness, knowing that 'the weakness of God is stronger than men' (1 Corinthians 1:25)—and so it proved to be.

Into the valley of Elah

And where did David go, alone and defenceless? He went down into the valley of Elah, that place between the two armies where Goliath held undisputed sway, and where none else dared to go. The women of Israel put their hands on their mouths and wept as they saw that slim youth walk, as it seemed, 'into the jaws of death, into the mouth of hell.' He was putting himself into a position where Goliath could triumph over him, and with that all Israel's hopes would disappear. How much was at stake that day!

And likewise with Jesus. Alone and defenceless, He went into the realm where Satan held sway, that realm of death which Satan had the legal right to inflict on sinners, and with Him went the hopes of all mankind. He could only render the devil powerless over man if He could take away from him that on which his power was based. To do that He must identify Himself not only with our humanity, but with our sins. As the old hymn says, 'He took my sins and my sorrows, He made them His very own.' And the moment He did that, the devil, who had been fastening on me, now fastened on Him, for the authority he had had over me he now had over Jesus. If he could conquer Him, the whole human race belonged to him, and there was no hope for any of us. Jesus was our only champion, and in taking responsibility for man's sin, He put Himself in the place where the devil, who had the power of death, had the right to inflict that death on Him.

He went in confidence

In spite of the awesome thing David was doing in going down into the valley of Elah, he went in complete confidence in the God of Israel, utterly sure of the issue. What a difference between Saul and David here! 'He's too big to hit,' was Saul's attitude. 'He's too big to miss,' was David's. In spite of the human odds against him, never was there a bolder assertion of faith, or a greater assurance of victory, than the words he spoke to Goliath in that valley. 'Thou comest to me with a sword, and with a spear, and with a shield but I come to thee in the name of the LORD of hosts, the God of the armies of Israel, whom thou hast defied. This day will the LORD deliver thee into mine hand; and I will smite thee, and take thine head from thee; and I will give the carcases of the host of the Philistines this day unto the fowls of the air, and to the wild beasts of the earth; that all the earth may know that there is a God in Israel.' Quite extraordinary!

But nothing like so extraordinary as the manner in which Jesus approached His conflict with the devil. As He entered the dark valley of Satan's power, He said, 'Now is the judgment of this world: now shall the prince of this world be cast out: and I, if I be lifted up from the earth, will draw all men unto me' (John 12:31–32). He was utterly confident of victory over His foe. But the battle was to be fought and won on a different principle from David's. He did not only say, 'I come to thee with no sword, spear, or shield'; but in effect He said, 'I do not even come to thee with a sling and stone. I will allow thee to inflict on Me that death due to sin which thou desirest to inflict on all the sons of men.' And Satan did it, and for three days he thought he had won—but only three days. The third day God raised Him from the dead, for in that death He had fully borne the judgment due to human sin and paid the ransom price to set Satan's captives free.

> If Jesus had not paid the debt,
> He ne'er had been at freedom set.

And what looked like defeat proved to be victory.

The story is told that when the news of the battle of Waterloo was relayed back to England, it was done by means of a heliograph, an instrument which could reflect the sun's rays over long distances, and transmit a message in morse code. The message began, 'Wellington defeated...,' and then a fog came down and interrupted the sentence. But it had got through to England, 'Wellington defeated,' and gloom spread everywhere, since they got just that part of the message and thought it was the whole. Disaster seemed to stare the nation in the face. In an hour or two the fog lifted and the sentence was completed: 'Napoleon at Waterloo.' And it really is true for you and me, that defeat has been turned to victory at Calvary.

Goliath slain with his own sword

And Jesus has done it by that very death which Satan thought was his *coup d'états*. Just as David cut off the head of Goliath with his own sword, for there was no sword of his own in David's hand, so Jesus, 'through death destroyed him that had the power of death, that is, the devil' (Hebrews 2:14):

> By weakness and defeat,
> He won the mead and crown,
> Trod all His foes beneath His feet
> By being trodden down.
>
> He hell in hell laid low,
> Made sin, He sin o'erthrew,
> Bowed to the grave destroyed it so,
> And death by dying slew.

In this way, the way of apparent weakness, was won

> That great victory o'er sin and death and woe,
> That needs no second fight,
> And leaves no second foe.

More than that, David's victory was every Israelite's victory that day. 'And when the Philistines saw their champion was dead, they fled. And the men of Israel and of Judah arose, and shouted, and pursued the Philistines, until thou come to the valley, and to the gates of Ekron.... And the children of Israel returned from chasing after the Philistines, and they spoiled their tents.' They entered into David's victory over Goliath and exploited it to the full on the Philistines.

Even so is this true of what the Lord Jesus has done for us. The New Testament verse I have quoted above does not end where I have ended it: '... that through death he might destroy him that had the power of death, that is, the devil;' it goes on to say, *and deliver them who through fear of death were all their lifetime subject to bondage* (Hebrews 2:15). Because of that work of His on the cross, there is no need for me to go around accused by Satan and feeling depressed. There is no need to listen for a moment to his whisper that there is no hope, that I might just as well indulge further in this or that sin, that I shall never get free, that he is stronger than I and so on. It is all a lie; I can be as free of guilt as Jesus is. The foes that He overcame were my foes. Remember that when you next sing the words, 'Up from the grave He arose, with a mighty triumph o'er His foes!' His foes were your foes. He fought them as your Surety. And if He is free of them now, so are you! And the way by which He was set free is the way by which you can be free—by His blood. Hebrews 13:20 tells us that He was 'brought again from the dead... through the blood of the everlasting covenant.' If the blood shed on Calvary was enough to bring from the dead the Surety, it is enough for all those for whom He stood surety. This was the great vision of the meaning of the victory of the cross which Charles Wesley had when he wrote,

> The reign of sin and death is o'er
> And all may live from sin set free:
> Satan hath lost his mortal power;
> 'Tis swallowed up in victory.

Goliath's armour in David's tent

Notice the verse: 'And David took the head of the Philistine, and brought it to Jerusalem; *but he put his armour in his tent*' (1 Samuel 17:54). As I read that sentence, I like to think of that dread armour which had terrified the Israelites, hanging as a trophy in David's tent.

And what shall we say of Satan's armour and weaponry, with which he has afflicted and terrified us for so long? They are just trophies in Jesus' tent; they can be things of the past for you. 'And having spoiled (RV 'put off from himself') principalities and powers, he made a show of them openly, triumphing over them in it' (Colossians 2:15). The principalities and powers were the Satanic forces that fastened on Him at the cross. Well, He has put them off now and displays openly their weaponry as harmless. The RSV translates it, 'He disarmed the principalities and powers.' That adds to the picture. In Christ Satan is a disarmed foe; we have died to sin's power to accuse, the law's power to condemn, and Satan's ability to rub it all in. The law has sentenced me to death; in Christ that sentence has already been carried out and I cannot be further accused. I need not then go on condemning myself, provided I go to Jesus and confess—and then believe in the mighty power of the blood of Jesus to set me free.

> For me, Lord Jesus, Thou hast died
>   And I have died in Thee;
> Thou'rt risen: my bands are all untied,
>   And now Thou liv'st in me.
> When purified, made white and tried
>   Thy glory then, for me!

All this the young anointed king, as yet unrecognized, did for Saul, the rejected king. The latter is still in the same condition, unwilling to accept the verdict of God on him, still unbroken. And yet what was done was for him as much as any other, and he benefited from it. He saw it and rejoiced (1 Samuel 19:5). It was so good to be free from the threat of Goliath. He was grateful to David, immensely so—at least, for a while. But the real struggle with his proud ego had scarcely begun. Very much as it is with us; we are glad of such experiences of salvation, but their purpose is to introduce us to God's deeper dealings with our proud ego too.

And Saul said, They have ascribed unto David ten thousands, and to me they have ascribed but thousands: and what can he have more but the kingdom? And Saul eyed David from that day and forward.

1 Samuel 18:8–9

4

The Jealousy of the Rejected King

We have seen so far two main things about Saul. First, he was the king whom God had rejected from reigning over Israel. Secondly, he was unwilling to accept that verdict, but carried on vainly in an office that God had declared him unfit for. Serious as it was for Saul to be rejected from being king, it was even more so that he refused to bow to that verdict and acknowledge the rightness of it. Had he accepted it and confessed that he was indeed unfit to rule and was ready to turn everything over to the one chosen to replace him, I am sure God would have shown mercy to a humbled, chastened man, and would have found some place for him in the kingdom. It might seem almost inconceivable that Saul would have taken such a step, but his unwillingness on this one point led him from one evil to another, until his life ended in stark tragedy, himself and his sons slain in battle and his own headless body impaled on the wall of a Philistine city. And all because he would not be broken—by which I mean he would not repent and accept God's verdict on himself.

One of the most terrible results of this unwillingness was that he became possessed by an insensate jealousy of David, to whom he owed so much as Israel's saviour, but

whom he found being preferred before him in the praises
of the people. The story of that growing jealousy, which
ultimately became almost pathological, is a long one. It
begins at chapter 18 and goes right through to chapter 31.
It makes frightening reading as to what jealousy can lead
to and underlines the urgency of our judging the first sign
of it in our hearts.

It all began with a trifle, that song of the women as
they celebrated Israel's victory over the Philistines, 'Saul
has slain his thousands, and David his ten thousands.'
But it was not a trifle to Saul. 'They have ascribed unto
David ten thousands,' he said, 'but to me but thousands.'
However, he would hardly have felt that jealousy had he
not been hanging on to a position from which God had
rejected him. When later the growing favour of David
with the people and God's obvious prospering of him on
the field of battle and elsewhere made it clear to Saul that
this was the man chosen of God to replace him, then there
was nothing he would not do to eliminate him. Whereas
he had been very glad to be saved by David from Goliath
and the Philistines, he was not willing to be supplanted
by him. And yet apart from this basic unwillingness on
Saul's part, his jealousy was quite irrational, as jealousy
so often is; David had done nothing to provoke him. As
Jonathan said, when expostulating with his father, 'Let not
the king sin against his servant, against David; because he
hath not sinned against thee, and because his works have
been to thee-ward very good' (1 Samuel 19:4). And from
that point the long story began. It is at bottom simply the
record of the unwillingness of the rejected king to bow to
the anointed one.

We pass on to the analogy as it applies to us. If we are unwilling to acknowledge ourselves as rejected kings and if we hang on to a throne God has declared us unfit for, we cannot but fall into jealousy sooner or later. And what a terrible thing it is! What hurts it causes to others and how much misery to ourselves! Jealousy is the only sin that gives us no pleasure. And how much more common is it among Christians than we in our naivety imagine. It is behind so many words, actions and attitudes, though often subtly camouflaged. And we blithely think we personally are innocent of it. I believe it could be said that the Christian who has not begun to see jealousy has hardly begun!

Jealous of Jesus?

But, you say, if Saul was jealous of David, are you suggesting that I am jealous of Jesus? Not in a direct way, but in an indirect manner, most certainly. You see, you are the rejected king; your kingdom has been rent from you and given to Jesus; He is to take your place. But He does not always seek to do that directly; He does it, as often as not, via somebody else. Somebody else excels us; somebody else is preferred before us; it looks as if that one will take over from us, and steal the limelight. Are you quite sure that it is not Jesus Who is showing us we are not what we thought, and Himself seeking to eclipse us and take our place? He sometimes does things that way, you know. John the Baptist said, 'He must increase, but I must decrease,' but He does not increase save at our expense, and the issue invariably arises with regard to another. We are jealous of that one and we resent and resist him. But in acting like that towards him we are acting thus to Jesus, and He has to say to us, 'Inasmuch as you have done it unto him, you have done it unto me.' This is, then, not something merely between us and another, as we have thought; it is rather something between us and Jesus and must be settled, if it is ever to be settled, on the basis that we have not been willing to be supplanted by Jesus. In wanting to be first with regard to another I have been wanting to be first with regard to Christ.

The progress of jealousy

May I ask you to note the progress of Saul's jealousy and how it expressed itself. Its first expression was *fear*. Three times in 1 Samuel 18, the chapter which tells of that unfortunate song of the women, we have the phrase, 'And Saul was afraid of David.' He felt threatened by the wisdom with which David conducted himself, by the way things always seemed to prosper in his hands, and by the favour of the people towards him. 'And what can he have more than the throne?' he said. Because his hold on the throne was so tenuous, it was easy for him to feel fearful of the man of whom he was jealous, though David never intended to be anything but his loyal servant.

Our jealousy invariably makes us feel threatened. Desiring at bottom only our own advancement, we are unwilling to accept with grace another's, seeing in it a possible challenge to our own. And we watch that other's every movement, just as 'Saul eyed David from that day and forward.' More than that, we take sly steps of our own to counter his.

Then came *suspicion*. Saul began to suspect that David

was conspiring against him behind his back. Every action of David's was looked upon in that light. And there were not wanting enemies of David to whisper in Saul's ear, 'David seeketh thy hurt.' And this close link between David and Jonathan, thought Saul darkly, what did it mean but that his own son was also involved in the plots? And not only Jonathan, but others also. He was surrounded by enemies! In modern psychological terms Saul became a paranoiac, mistakenly feeling that everyone was against him. Said Saul to his servants one day, 'All of you have conspired against me, and there is none that showeth me that my son hath made a league with the son of Jesse, *and there is none of you that is sorry for me*, or showeth unto me that my son hath stirred up my servant against me, to lie in wait, as at this day' (1 Samuel 22:8). There speaks the paranoiac with characteristic irrationality. Some of the modern dictators and tyrants are like that. Feeling themselves threatened, and suspecting everybody they say, 'None of you is sorry for me!' We ought to be sorry for their victims, not for them! Yes, 'uneasy lies the head that wears the crown,' especially when that crown has been filched and never ought to be on that head at all. We must beware lest that unrepented jealousy of ours lead us in one degree or another into that stage when we begin to suspect those of whom we are jealous and see evil where none is intended.

Then all this led Saul on quite naturally to open *hostility* to David. Because he thought David was his enemy, he felt it only self-defence to take up a like attitude to David. And so 'Saul became David's enemy continually,' and expressed it in the most open and outrageous acts. Look at the long list of his vicious perpetrations against this innocent young man. On no less than three occasions he cast a javelin at him, as David played his harp to comfort him in his demonic depressions. Then, in giving him his daughter Michal to wife, he asked for a savage dowry—a hundred foreskins of the Philistines—in the hope that David would embroil himself with them and be slain. That failing, he commanded Jonathan and his servants to kill David, which only drew forth remonstrances from Jonathan. Then one night Saul got his men to surround David's house to slay him in the morning, but he escaped just in time. Then Jonathan found himself the object of Saul's hatred because of his espousal of David's cause and narrowly missed Saul's javelin. Oh, that javelin again, a dangerous weapon in the hands of a man like Saul!

It thus became clear that David must leave the court completely, and live the life of an exile in hiding. Thereafter he dwelt 'in deserts, and in mountains, and in dens and caves of the earth' as Hebrews 1 puts it, with a few hundred men, likewise ill-satisfied with Saul, a sort of Old Testament Robin Hood. Perhaps his greatest grief at this point was to hear that the priests, who in all innocence had given him temporary shelter at one time, had been slain by Saul, seventy-five of them—only one escaped to tell the tale. David broke his heart as he said, 'I have occasioned the death of all the persons of thy father's household.' As he moved from hiding place to hiding place, he found his whereabouts were betrayed to Saul, first by the inhabitants of Keilah and then by those of Ziph, in spite of the fact that in the case of the former he had done them costly service. Saul mobilized three thousand men to hunt him like a 'partridge in the mountains,' to use David's own phrase. It was, as we should say today, 'a cat and mouse' chase, with the chances weighted all in favour of the cat, except that God was on the side of the mouse. Three breath-taking incidents in the wildernesses of Maon, Engedi and Ziph are told in great detail, occasions when there was, to use David's words again, 'but a step between me and death.' But all the time there was a protecting hand over David. His faith in the God Who had first anointed him, so often expressed in the psalms he wrote at this time, was amply vindicated. 'And Saul sought him every day, but God delivered him not into his hands.'

Our jealousy, too, can sometimes lead us along the same course; first fear, then suspicion, and finally open hostility. Imagining the other person is working against us, it will seem to us only self defence to work against them. Quite outrageous words and acts can be said and done against others as a result—even in our churches. And the suffering we inflict on others can be very great.

Reading the story as just so much history, we can overlook how keenly David felt his treatment at the hands of Saul. It was a deeply affecting moment, when realizing it was not safe for him to remain at the court and that he must go where he could, David and Jonathan, 'wept one with another, until David exceeded.' David, I imagine, hid his face on Jonathan's shoulder while sobs shook that young body. 'What have I done?' he asked. 'What is mine iniquity? And what is my sin before thy father, that he seeketh my life?' He might well ask, for jealousy is so often insatiable; nothing will pacify it. We have to look at some of the psalms he wrote under these trials to understand how deeply he felt them.

We know too little what suffering we have inflicted on others. The words we spoke did not cause the other to react much at the time, and he seemed to take it quietly, but the wound went deep; he went over it again and again in his mind and it caused him great unhappiness. For instance, the members of a church little know that their criticism of their minister has sometimes caused him and his wife to cry themselves to sleep at night. Be assured, God is the avenger of all such, as He was of David. Inasmuch as we have done it to another, we have done it to the Lord Jesus. Looked at in that way, the treatment we have accorded Him is no better than that which Saul meted out to David, and He has suffered as much. I once heard a friend pray a very simple, but deep prayer. 'Lord Jesus,' he said, 'it has been very hard for Thee to be our Saviour.' Hard, indeed. He has so often been 'wounded in the house of His friends.'

David not against Saul

The man whom Saul thought was against him was not against him at all. None loved him more than David did, nor any respected his position as the Lord's anointed more than he. Twice he had Saul completely at his mercy and he could so easily have pierced him to the ground as he lay asleep. But he refused to do so. In the one instance when Saul was hunting David, he came into a cave to escape the sun and have a midday sleep, little knowing that deeper in that very cave David and his men were hiding. His men thought it was a God-given chance for David to avenge himself of his enemy and thus end his troubles. But he stayed his servants with the words, 'The LORD forbid that I should do this thing unto my master, the LORD's anointed.' So he merely cut off the skirt of Saul's robe, though he had qualms of conscience about doing even that. But he needed something to demonstrate to Saul the innocence of his intentions.

The second incident was two chapters later when David and Abishai crept down one night into Saul's camp while he lay asleep, and David stood over him as he lay helpless at his feet. Abishai begged permission to put an end to him, but David said the same again. 'Destroy him not; for who can stretch his hand against the LORD's anointed and be guiltless?' He simply removed Saul's spear and cruse of water as evidence of his midnight visit. And when eventually Saul was slain in battle by the Philistines, none mourned for Saul as David did. 'The beauty of Israel is slain upon thy high places: how are the mighty fallen! Tell it not in Gath, publish it not in the streets of Askelon... Saul and Jonathan were lovely and pleasant in their lives, and in their death they were not divided: they were swifter than eagles, they were stronger than lions.' (2 Samuel 1:19–23.) This was the man whom Saul thought was against him and whom he therefore hunted. How wrong can you be?

This pictures the One Whom you think, in the person of others, is against you, and Whom you are therefore opposing—and all because of jealousy, which in turn is because you will not accept the many evidences that you are the rejected king, the failure whom Jesus must replace by Himself. Dear brother, sister, you are loved, and that by the very One you have so wronged. You are an enemy, but a beloved enemy, though the more He loves the less He be loved. Many waters cannot quench His love for you, neither can the floods drown it.

As David held up the evidence of his love for Saul, that torn skirt, he pleaded with Saul to put away his unthinking hatred, saying, 'Wherefore, hearest thou men's words, saying, Behold, David seeketh thy hurt? Behold, this day thine eyes have seen how that the LORD had delivered thee today into mine hand in the cave: and some bade me kill thee: but mine eye spared thee.' Perhaps we can put these words into the mouth of Jesus as He pleads with us to repent. We have lain at His feet, defenceless and helpless, oblivious of this and that danger that has come near us. Heavenly intelligences have wondered at His tolerance of our ways and His patience with our intransigence, and they bade Him kill us, and none could have charged Him with injustice had He done so. But He says to us, 'Mine eye spared thee, spared thee more times than thou knowest.' Indeed, He has showered us with kindnesses utterly beyond our deservings. And if that argument prevails not with us, He points to His scars received on Calvary for us, and says, 'Some bade Me kill thee, but I not only spared thee, but died for thee.'

Those who suffer the wrong

What shall we say to those who suffer wrong at the hands of jealousy? Sometimes we are on the receiving side of this terrible thing. We have a Saul who plays the part of an enemy to us, and nothing we do seems able to mollify him or her. We ask their forgiveness for this or that, anything in which we think we might have offended them, but it makes no difference. Sometimes they will not even tell us what it is they have against us, and we cannot imagine what it can be. Whenever there is such a hostile attitude in another which nothing seems to pacify, I think you are right to say it is jealousy. In that case there is nothing you can do—except bear it with Jesus. He suffered at the hands of jealousy; it was the jealousy of the priests that put Him on the cross; you are in good company, then, when you suffer it too. You may, of course, get wrong in your own attitude in the process of bearing it; you may have self-pity, feel resentment or frustration. Just put that right with the Lord as you go, realizing that this suffering is a yoke He has given you to bear with Him.

And yet I think there is something that might be done. If there is no one else to do it, you might have to do it yourself. You might say what David said, and that boldly, eyeball to eyeball. David held up that torn skirt, evidence that he had no evil intentions against Saul, and said, 'The LORD judge between me and thee, and the LORD avenge me of thee: but mine hand shall not be upon thee' (1 Samuel 24:12). I think it is right sometimes to say, 'May the Lord be judge between you and me, and may the Lord avenge me of you. I leave it to Him to do it.' Yes, I feel you can use the word 'avenge,' as long as you are not doing the avenging. After all, the Lord Himself says, 'Vengeance is mine; I will repay.' It could lead that other person to recover himself. If you said that to me, I am not sure that I would like it to be left for the Lord to avenge you of me; He did it on some in Scripture, He might do it again. I have known one or two cases where some such challenge has led to the person's repentance. But you must guard your spirit; it must be as loving as was David's.

Saul nearly repents

What effect did all this have on Saul, and how did it end
with him? David's attitude and action in these two incidents quite melted Saul and it looked as if he was going to
capitulate to God. I quote his words after the first incident
(1 Samuel 24:16–21):

And it came to pass, when David had made an end of speaking
these words unto Saul, that Saul said, Is this thy voice, my son
David? And Saul lifted up his voice, and wept. And he said to
David, Thou art more righteous than I: for thou hast rewarded
me good, whereas I have rewarded thee evil. And thou hast
showed this day that thou hast dealt well with me: forasmuch as
when the LORD had delivered me into thine hand, thou killedst
me not. For if a man find his enemy, will he let him go well
away? Wherefore the LORD reward thee good for that thou hast
done unto me this day. And now, behold. I know well that thou
shalt surely be king, and that the kingdom of Israel shall be
established in thine hand. Swear now therefore unto me by the
LORD, that thou wilt not cut off my seed after me, and that thou
wilt not destroy my name out of my father's house.

Not only does he confess that David has been right and
he wrong, but he concedes that one day David will be
king, and he asks that David should swear to spare his
seed in that day. What an extraordinary situation—it is not
the runaway exile pleading with the king to save his life,
but the king pleading with the exile to spare his seed. We
think we are hearing at last the response we have waited
so long for, but which we had thought to be inconceivable.
But, alas, the old enmity broke out again, and David was
once more in peril.

Then follows that second incident when David spared

Saul, and here Saul seems to get much nearer to repentance. Indeed, we ask ourselves, could a man really say more?

Then said Saul, I have sinned: return, my son David: for I will no more do thee harm, because my soul was precious in thine eyes this day: behold, I have played the fool, and have erred exceedingly.... Blessed be thou, my son David: thou shalt both do great things, and also shalt still prevail. (1 Samuel 26:21, 25)

But in spite of Saul's invitation for him to return to the court, David did not do so. 'So David went on his way, and Saul returned to his place.' David did not dare return with him. He knew the basic situation had not changed. What was needed was not merely a conceding that David should be king one day in the future, but that he should be king right there and then. Not that David was pressing for that, but he knew until the rejected king had repented there he would not be safe; Saul's repentance was only partial.

The point of no return

Thereafter Saul seemed to pass the point of no return, for he hastened on his downward path to disaster. With the Philistines massing for the final assault, he found he could not turn to the Lord, or rather, when he tried to do so, he got no answer. 'And when Saul inquired of the LORD, the LORD answered him not, neither by dreams, nor by Urim, nor by prophets.' There was too much standing between the Lord and Saul for God to talk to him about the immediate battle. There were other things the Lord would want to raise first, but Saul was in no mood for that. And so he said, 'Seek me a woman that hath a familiar spirit, that I may go to her, and inquire of her.' The witch of Endor was what we would call today a spiritualist medium, who like the witches of old have, I understand, a familiar spirit, a control spirit, by which they get in touch with the world of demons. Saul's hope was somehow to get in touch with Samuel by her means.

This is ever the background story of those who turn to spiritism and the occult. 'Should not a people seek unto their God? for the living should they seek to the dead?' (Isaiah 8:19). Yes, of course they should turn to their God, but, like Saul, they have so many sins which they will need to confess to Him that they prefer to 'seek unto them that have familiar spirits, and unto wizards that peep, and that mutter.' With them there is no need to face moral issues, as there is with the living God.

It may be asked, did Saul really communicate with the dead through that medium? My answer is yes and no. Normally she was never able to communicate with the dead. Her claim to do so was bogus, as are the claims of present day mediums. What occurs today is either a deception on the part of the medium, or, more likely, a deception of the devil himself, who impersonates the dead. I do not think, then, the woman ever expected to bring up Samuel. She was resorting to her usual hocus pocus by which she had deceived so many, when suddenly she saw Samuel, and 'she cried with a loud voice.' In other words, she was more surprised than anyone—and terrified. This was the real thing in a way it had never been before. It was God Himself doing it this time. And when Samuel spoke to Saul it was on the old moral issues with which he had faced him long before.

And Samuel said to Saul. Why hast thou disquieted me, to bring me up? And Saul answered, I am sore distressed; for the Philistines make war against me, and God is departed from me, and answereth me no more. Then said Samuel, Wherefore then dost thou ask of me, seeing the LORD is departed from thee, and is become thine enemy? Because thou obeyedst not the voice of the LORD, nor executedst his fierce wrath upon Amalek, therefore hath the LORD done this thing unto thee this day. (1 Samuel 28:15–18)

Not this way do the supposed spirits of the dead speak in séances today, or in any before.

From that visit Saul received nothing but a confirmation of his doom. The battle was joined, the Israelites fled before the Philistines and many were slain on Mount Gilboa. Jonathan, too, was killed, together with Saul's two other sons, while Saul himself was wounded by the archers. Rather than allow himself to fall into the hands of the Philistines and be abused by them, Saul took a sword and fell upon it, thus killing himself. His head was cut off and his body fastened to the wall of Bethshan, while the Philistines rejoiced. A dark day for Israel!

Thus ends the story of the man who would not be broken. Had his been a broken and a contrite heart, which in the sight of God is of great price, it would have ended so differently. At all sorts of points in the story the place of repentance on his part and mercy on God's was available to him. But the cost of self-humbling made him postpone his chance again and again, until eventually there was no remedy.

And Jonathan Saul's son arose, and went to David into the wood... and he said unto him... Thou shalt be king over Israel, and I shall be next unto thee.

1 Samuel 23:16–17

5

Jonathan and the Cure of Jealousy

If Saul was the man who was not willing to be broken, there was another in the story who was more than willing. It was Jonathan. As Saul's son and the next in line to the throne, he had as much to lose as his father by David's presence on the scene. Saul told him as much one day in a fit of rage: 'Thou hast chosen the son of Jesse to thine own confusion.... For as long as the son of Jesse liveth upon the ground, thou shalt not be stablished, nor thy kingdom.' And yet if it meant choosing him 'to his own confusion,' he chose him nonetheless. From their first meeting on the day that David came back from his triumph over Goliath, the soul of Jonathan was knit with the soul of David, and he loved him as his own soul. They made a covenant of friendship together that day, and as a seal Jonathan stripped himself of his robe, sword, bow and girdle, and gave them to David. And he remained loyal to that bond to the end, no matter what trouble it caused between his father and himself. But Jonathan went further than this. It is quite clear that Jonathan was willing to accept himself as part of a rejected house and to let David be king in God's appointed time. An important passage here is that which tells how one day he went to his fugitive friend in the wood 'and strengthened his hand

in God.' He then went on to utter words which are surely
the noblest in the whole narrative: 'Fear not: for the hand
of Saul my father shall not find thee; and *thou shalt be
king over Israel, and I shall be next unto thee*; and that
also Saul my father knoweth' (1 Samuel 23:17). He said
in effect that he was so sure that God had appointed David
to be king, that he would never for a moment contest his
kingship, and that the most that he would ask for himself
was simply to be next to David. What words to hear from
the heir apparent to the throne: 'Thou shalt be king and
I will be next unto thee.' The very opposite of Saul's
attitude! No jealousy here—just love!

Then again the two of them made a covenant together in
fuller terms than before, terms which are really quite surprising. It is not the fugitive pleading for favours from his
friend at court, but rather the other way round. So certain
is Jonathan that David will be king, that he asks first that
when that day arrives David will show him the kindness
of the Lord, that he die not at his hand; and secondly (and
more importantly) that after he is gone David will not cut
off his kindness from his house, that is his seed, forever.
Usually a new king would liquidate all the remnants of
the former line. Jonathan asks David to swear that it shall
not be so, because of their love for one another. And all
this is said to a fugitive who has no human possibility of
ever being a king. What an attitude was this of Jonathan's
to David! The only similar attitude that occurs to me is
that of the dying thief, who, turning to that One dying on
a cross like his with nothing about Him to suggest that
He was a king entering a kingdom, said to Him, 'Lord,
remember me when thou comest into thy kingdom.' What

a revelation from the Holy Spirit that dying thief was given as to Who was on the next-door cross.

Next

'Thou shalt be king and I shall be *next* unto thee.' What a great little word that is, *next*! Only a man in whom the Holy Spirit is working can really say it. The natural thing for us all is to want to be *first*—especially with regard to others, and what disharmony and jealousy that causes!

But, as we have seen, first with regard to others means first with regard to the Lord Jesus. But when convicted of this we say, 'Jesus, You be first; I'm willing to be next,' that means next in our other relationships too! Next with regard to Jesus and next with regard to my brother always go together. 'Let each esteem other better than himself (Philippians 2:3). That does not mean necessarily better in abilities or qualities but in position, just as a servant esteems the master better in position than himself. And when we are willing to regard ourselves next, then with love we will serve one another.

Next, next, next—that is the cure of jealousy. Next, because I have accepted God's verdict on myself as a rejected king and am willing for Jesus to be first. 'Thou shalt be King and I shall be next unto Thee.' When darts of jealousy come in with regard to another, I must learn to repent and take my place quickly as 'next.'

How sweet Christian fellowship is when it is a whole group of 'nexts,' working and praying together with only one person who is first, and that is Jesus! It is a fellowship of mutual 'nextness' and there is no jealousy there.

He never forgot

What was it that prevailed on Jonathan to take this attitude to David and resign his crown-rights to him? I believe he never forgot that day when he saw David coming back from the valley of Elah, carrying the head of Goliath in his hand. He expressed the memory of it when he said to his father, 'He did put his life in his hand and slew the Philistine, and the LORD wrought a great salvation for all Israel: thou sawest it and didst rejoice.' But for David there would have been no kingdom to contend over, and he would have been a slave to the Philistines. This young champion had saved him and all Israel from such servitude. He owed him every breath he drew. 'Me be king?' we can imagine him saying. 'Not when David is around! Let him be king—I'll just be next.'

It is the vision of the cross that prevails on us to give up our place and take the position of only next to Him and to others. We are never to forget how the Lamb of God took His life in His hand, how He went for us into that realm where sin and Satan ruled, the realm of judgment, and defeated our foe by giving up Himself. I would not have a throne to yield up, but for what He did for me there.

> Lord, bend that proud and stiff-necked I;
> Help me to bow the head and die,
> Beholding Him on Calvary,
> Who bowed His head for me.

It is, however, not only appreciation of His work on the cross that is to motivate me, but supremely personal attachment to Him in love. Jonathan loved David as his own soul. When John the Baptist first saw Jesus he said, 'Behold, the Lamb of God, which taketh away the sin of the world' (John 1:29). The next day his cry was a little different, just 'Behold the Lamb of God!' (verse 36). The first day it was His work, that of taking away the sins of the world. The next day it was just His person that preoccupied him: 'Behold the Lamb of God!' That is something of growing in grace. The readiness with which I 'bow the head and die' is the degree in which I am attached to the Lamb of God Himself.

Saul or a Jonathan?

So we have these two contrasted characters, Saul and Jonathan, and we may well ask ourselves, am I a Saul, or a Jonathan? In a matter like this I find I have to approach the positive via the negative. By that I mean, that to become a Jonathan I am not to ask to be made such, but simply to confess that I am a Saul. I have to confess that I have been a king in my own right, that I have wanted to be first, not next, that I have been jealous and so on. I am to come via the negative, because the first thing I need is not to make a new consecration, but to be forgiven; and the condition for forgiveness is confession. Here we must not hurry. It is as if God says, 'Don't try to be a Jonathan. Don't even ask Me to make you one. Just acknowledge how deeply you are a Saul, let Me show you all.' And strangely, this is the way to become a Jonathan. For at the cross of Jesus where such confession is made, something always happens, and you emerge not only forgiven, but with a new attitude, a Jonathan saying, 'He now is King, and I only next to Him.' And if again Saul becomes apparent in you, and he

doubtless will, you know where to go and what to do—
and you do it, and praise Him again. Even if it means
confessing to Jesus jealous thoughts and attitudes several
times a day, you can still praise Him, for His blood has
never lost its power to restore joy to the repenting soul.
The paradoxical thing is that victory over jealousy and
love for others come not by repenting less and less, but
ever more frequently and more quickly. Remember, the
windscreen in your car is only clear in rain while the wiper
is going back and forth continually. And you do need to
repent—you are the rejected king! Who are you to want to
be first? Next is your true place. The first is His.

On a visit to East Africa years ago I heard an African
woman (who was largely illiterate) say in a fellowship
meeting something very profound. She said God had
shown her that when she was jealous it was only because
she wanted to be at the head of the queue, but that when
she repented of it, she went to the end of the queue, and
there she always found Jesus. Quite so, because that is
where He went at Calvary, to the lowest and last place
in the line. And though He is now highly exalted above
every other, He still manages to be at the end of the queue
to meet you when you go there. It then becomes a matter
of indifference to you who is at the head of the line; you
have found again your true place next to Him. What a
joy! And so it is that if jealousy is the only sin that gives
no pleasure, repentance of jealousy seems to bring more
blessing to the heart than repentance of any other sin, for
in going to that last place we always find Jesus Himself
there. And by the power of His blood we are cleansed
from the stain of that sin and put completely right with

God again.

Then sometimes He says, 'Friend, come up higher.' But even then it is only to be the more next to Him.

And David said, Is there yet any that is left of the house of Saul, that I may show him kindness for Jonathan's sake?

2 Samuel 9:1

6

The Magnanimity of the Anointed King

We come now to that part of the story when Saul and his sons have fallen in battle at the hands of the Philistines, and when David at last is made king. For the first seven-and-a-half years he had reigned only over Judah, living in Hebron, but now by popular acclaim he was made king over all Israel, and he continued as such for a long reign of forty years in all.

His first act on being made king was to secure the city of Jebus for himself, ousting its inhabitants and changing its name to Jerusalem. Then in a series of victorious battles he subdued the Philistines by whom the country had been overrun in the days of Saul. That done, he brought the ark of the covenant from the house of Abinadab, where it had lain on the periphery of the nation all the days of Saul, right to the central place in Jerusalem, symbolic of his earnest desire that God should now be the centre of the nation's life.

Then, with himself established on the throne, the Philistines subdued and the ark brought to Jerusalem, he addressed himself to a matter that had been on his heart from the very moment he became king. 'And David said,

Is there yet any that is left of the house of Saul, that I may show him kindness for Jonathan's sake?' Then follows a story of such magnanimity that it shines like the sun on the pages of the Old Testament, a magnanimity that can only be likened to that which God extends to sinners. The words grace and magnanimity, of course, mean virtually the same. The former word is perhaps over-familiar to us and might as a result lack freshness; it is good, then, to speak sometimes of the magnanimity of God. When I have been preaching in a German-speaking country and have used this word, I have heard my interpreter translate it *Grossherzlichkeit*, that is, great-heartedness. And how vast is the great-heartedness of God, all the vaster when its recipients have no claim upon it, but rather deserve the reverse. Well, you have this illustrated here in a moving manner.

The theme, then, of this chapter of our book is the magnanimity which the anointed king showed to the house of the rejected king, when at last it was broken in defeat. It is this characteristic in David which makes him so attractive in our eyes. Its importance to us is that it pictures the magnanimity of Jesus Christ to His enemies, when at last they concede defeat. This grace is without end and delights to heap benefits without number on the heads of those who once opposed Him. It is the only basis on which we can have a new life in God at all, and we must never cease to marvel at it.

The object of David's magnanimity was Mephibosheth, the crippled son of Jonathan, the only one of the house of Saul to be found. The incident is told in 2 Samuel 9. It is the story of a banqueting table at which David was head and at which this man, the only descendant of the house of Saul, was given an honoured place, in spite of the deep hurts that house had inflicted on David. He is sitting there every day at the king's table, 'as one of the king's sons.' The forfeited lands of his father have been restored to him and he is given a company of servants to look after both his lands and his own personal needs. It was an unheard of thing, to receive into the family a son of a deposed king and a potential pretender to the throne. But David did it.

Before we look in detail at this and make its New Testament application to ourselves, I want you to look at the story of another table, years before, a table at which Saul was the head, when Saul treated David very differently from the way David later on was to treat his last remaining descendant. What a contrast we shall find between the table of which Saul was head and the table at which David was head.

So David hid himself in the field: and when the new moon was come, the king sat him down to eat meat. And the king sat upon his seat, as at other times, even upon a seat by the wall: and Jonathan arose, and Abner sat by Saul's side, and David's place was empty. Nevertheless Saul spake not anything that day: for he thought, Something hath befallen him, he is not clean; surely he is not clean. And it came to pass on the morrow, which was the second day of the month, that David's place was empty: and Saul said unto Jonathan his son, Wherefore cometh not the son of Jesse to eat meat, neither yesterday, nor today? And Jonathan answered Saul, David earnestly asked leave of me to go to Bethlehem: and he said, let me go, I pray thee; for our family hath a sacrifice in the city; and my brother, he hath commanded me to be there: and now, if I have found favour in thine eyes, let me get away, I pray thee, and see my brethren.

Therefore he cometh not unto the king's table. Then Saul's anger was kindled against Jonathan, and he said unto him, Thou son of a perverse, rebellious woman, do not I know that thou hast chosen the son of Jesse to thine own confusion...? For as long as the son of Jesse liveth upon the ground, thou shalt not be established, nor thy kingdom. Wherefore now send and fetch him unto me, for he shall surely die. And Jonathan answered Saul his father, and said unto him, Wherefore shall he be slain? what hath he done? And Saul cast a javelin at him to smite him: whereby Jonathan knew that it was determined of his father to slay David. So Jonathan arose from the table in fierce anger, and did eat no meat the second day of the month: for he was grieved for David, because his father had done him shame. (1 Samuel 20:24–34)

Saul at the head of the table

Let us look first at Saul at the head of the table, and let us recapitulate a little. Although God has rejected him from reigning over Israel, he will not accept that verdict but is still trying to be king, and as such he sits at the head. All the most important people are at the royal banquet and Saul, of course, is in the most prominent place.

We have already seen Saul to be a picture of ourselves. The verdict of the cross has gone out against us. Jesus not only died for us, but as us. This means we have been judged on that cross, and God has declared He has rejected us from reigning over the territory He has given us and has given it to the Neighbour of ours, Who is better than we. But like Saul, we will not accept that verdict. If we repent at all, we do not go to the depths of saying that that shows us to be failures, unfit to rule for God. That is too humiliating for us. We are sure we can yet be a success at being kings, if we really try. We are not going to stand down in favour of anybody else, not even Jesus. We are right; it is the others who are wrong. And there we are sitting in the central place at the head of the table.

The basic sin

Now this sin, being at the head of the table, is the basic sin from which all other sins spring. Take the sin of pride—what is it but me at the head of the table? What is the sin of jealousy but the same thing? I want to be at the head of the table and I am jealous of anybody who gets there instead of me. Resentment and bitterness towards others come also from the same source. People must respect my rights, and I resent it when they don't, but rather wrong me, as I imagine. And because I am at the head of the table, I harbour it in my mind and will not forgive them. Even the grosser sins are the result of this same basic attitude—sins such as dishonesty, or sexual impurity. If we, like Saul, are at the head of the table, why shouldn't we indulge? Why should we be strictly honest? And so, provided we are not likely to be found out, we transgress.

David's place empty

Then notice that because Saul was at the head of the table, David's place was empty. More than once in those verses you have that phrase, 'David's place was empty.' Everybody else was on parade that day. All the other important people and military leaders were there, but the most successful and the most loved of them all was not. He did not dare to come. It was more than his life was worth for David to sit at that table with Saul. There was always that javelin near at hand. It had been used before; it might be used again. David just could not sit at a table where Saul was head. And Saul did not like it. It is true he had no love for David, but he wanted him there if only to minister to his importance. Saul just could not get over that empty place each day.

And so it is with us. When we are at the head of the table, acting and reacting as *we* like, Jesus' place is empty. He cannot sit at our table when we are at the head. He has already received so much hurt from us, for inasmuch as we have acted as we have to others, we have done it unto Him. Can He sit at the table with such a man as that? And so He withdraws His presence, and we are left to try to live the Christian life without Him. We have to undertake Christian service with David's place empty. We can even be speaking about Him to others, preaching the gospel, teaching a Bible class, with all the time David's place empty. It is a terrible experience. I know because it has sometimes been mine. When the Lord first met my heart in revival, I had been engaged for years in evangelistic work, but latterly something had gone wrong, and I found myself trying to be an evangelist with David's place empty, without His presence and power with me. I was standing up in front of crowds, trying to persuade them to accept Jesus Christ, but all the time David's place was empty. I do not know what would have happened to me had not Jesus come again to me in revival. And there have been other occasions since, when my attitudes have been wrong, when I have opposed a brother, or been jealous of him, and then tried to serve the Lord, but David's place was empty and, of course, little or nothing happened—

except that I got more and more strained. It is hard work being at the head of the table, trying to be king, when God has already rejected you from being king.

From defeat to defeat

More than that, under Saul, the country staggered from one defeat to another, till it became a virtual vassal state of the Philistines. And yet all the time there was one among them, not only uniquely gifted in himself to lead Israel's forces, but the very one by whom God had promised to save His people. But Saul insisted on keeping things in his own hands; so in more ways than one David's place was empty.

We, too, go from defeat to defeat while we remain at the head of the table, unwilling to confess our wrong and keeping things in our own hands. And all the time there is One waiting so near, of Whom it is said, 'and the pleasure of the LORD shall prosper in His hand' (Isaiah 53–10). But things are not in His hands, they are in ours. How different everything would be if they were all in His hands! But we are unwilling to step down from the head of the table and things go from bad to worse: while His place is empty.

David at the head of the table

I know I have been over much of this ground in one or two previous chapters, but I have covered it again because I want to put this banqueting table in contrast with that other one, of which David was head. To find that story we have to turn a long way on, to the second book of Samuel, chapter 9. What a different scene we have here! Years have passed and the unbelievable has happened.

That very young man, once a persecuted exile, is now made king over all Israel. Saul has been slain in battle, his house and lineage have been broken, and his lands have been forfeited. To David's great sorrow Jonathan too has fallen in battle. David is now at the head of the table, king at last. And one of his first acts is to say those wonderful words, 'Is there yet any that is left of the house of Saul, that I may show him kindness for Jonathan's sake?'

For a king to say, is there any left of the house of the previous king, was quite usual. The first act of a king would be to eliminate all the former line, so that there would be none to challenge his right to the throne. So when they heard him say, 'Is there yet any that is left of the house of Saul...' they thought this was his purpose. What was their astonishment when he completed the sentence, '...that I may show him kindness for Jonathan's sake.' This was not after the manner of kings! But there had been a covenant between David and Jonathan, and David had promised that he would not 'cut off his kindness' to Jonathan's seed after him. So it was that when he came to the throne he enquired if there were any left of that poor, broken house, because he wanted to extend kindness to him for Jonathan's sake.

It was found that there was but one left, a cripple lame on both his feet and—what delighted David—he was a son of Jonathan. In 2 Samuel 4:4 we read that at the time of his father's death in the battle of Mount Gilboa, sixteen years before, he was a child of five. When news of the disastrous defeat and of Jonathan's death reached home, 'his nurse took him up, and fled: and it came to pass, as she made haste to flee, that he fell, and became lame. And his name was Mephibosheth.' This was doubtless particularly touching to David. Mephibosheth was not only a son of Jonathan, but he was crippled largely as a result of his father's death, which David had so deeply lamented. So it was he said immediately, 'Send and fetch him.'

David never acted so much like God, as when he treated Mephibosheth in the way he did. Moreover, David knew he was acting like God, and wanted to do so, because two verses later he says, '...that I may show the kindness of God unto him.' Here it is not only 'kindness' as in verse 1, but a certain sort of kindness, 'the kindness of God.' David had tasted that kindness when God took him from following the sheep, led him through all those troublous years, delivered him from his enemies and put him on a throne he did not deserve; and he longed to show that same kindness to the house of Saul. What a different scene we have here compared to that other table of which Saul was head!

It is even so with the sinner, or the failing saint. Once he is broken to acknowledge his wrong and to accept himself as the rejected king, the scene always changes. Instead of it being a table of which he is the head, it becomes a table of which the God of grace is the head, and He sits there to show kindness to His one-time foes. Although we have excluded Jesus from our table, He has reserved a place for us at His. Magnanimous treatment indeed!

So this story is one of the most graphic illustrations of the grace of God in Scripture. Grace is the undeserved love of God, with special emphasis on the *undeserved.* In the second chapter of Paul's letter to Titus (verse 11) we have the words, 'For the grace of God that bringeth salvation hath appeared to all men.' Then in the next chapter (verses 4–5) that grace is defined as 'the kindness and love of God our Saviour toward man, not by works of righteousness which we have done.' This beautiful element in the divine character is further explained in Paul's letter to the Romans (11:6) 'And if by grace, then is it no more of works; otherwise grace is no more grace.' If grace, then, is to be grace, the object of it must be undeserving and in misery, and Mephibosheth certainly qualified on these counts.

An enemy

First, he was an enemy; he belonged to that enemy house that had inflicted so many wrongs on David, and he had a potential claim to the throne. But David said, 'Enemy or not, I am going to show him kindness.'

And we personally have played the part of an enemy to God's Son; we have been unwilling to be supplanted by Him, and by our attitudes have virtually driven Him from our table. But enemy or not, God is determined to show us kindness. Although we have driven His Son from our table, He has found a place for us at His.

Lame on both his feet

Not only was Mephibosheth part of that enemy house, he was unattractive as regards his person, for he was a cripple, lame on both feet. It was a pitiful sight to see this man trying to walk. And yet David said, 'Cripple or not, I am going to show him kindness and he is going to sit at my table as one of the king's sons.'

We too are lame on both our feet, lame through the fall of Adam. Haven't you found that you are crippled? I certainly have. Usually it is on one foot more than the other. One foot is called promises, and I can make some wonderful promises. But the other foot is called performance, and that is the one that is lame. The thing I promise to do, I don't do, and the thing I promise never to do again, that I do. Paul suffered from this lameness. But you can be crippled on the other foot too—you feel you can't make any more promises, as you've broken so many in the past. We are all of us in this—a great company of Mephibosheths. But God says, 'Lame as they are, I am going to show them kindness.'

No bread

A third thing about Mephibosheth was that he was said to be living in a place called Lodebar, which in Hebrew means 'no bread.' It was a place where the experience of famine came to be normal, for the harvest never seemed to ripen there. And in living in such a place, Mephibosheth was living in utter poverty, with nothing to satisfy his hunger. 'I don't care where he lives,' said David, 'whether in Lodebar or anywhere else—I'm going to show him kindness that he has never imagined possible.' We too are objects of divine grace, just because we live in Lodebar, miserable, dissatisfied and empty. Were it otherwise grace would not be grace. And so it is God says, 'Even if you live in Lodebar, I'm going to show you a kindness that will more than meet your need and will transform life for you.'

For Jonathan's sake

Most important of all, this magnanimity, this kindness, was to be shown to Mephibosheth for Jonathan's sake. For David the whole house of Saul, which had caused him so much pain, was redeemed by his love for Jonathan.

Mephibosheth might have wondered how he could be sure of receiving this immense favour in the first place, and whether it would always continue towards him. How did he know that David would not weary of him one day? Most important of all, how could he be sure that ultimately he would not be dealt with as all pretenders were usually dealt with? All such fears were silenced when Mephibosheth heard David say, 'Fear not; I will surely show thee kindness for Jonathan thy father's sake.' Doubtless he had been told by those who brought him up what his father had meant to David in the early days, and of the bond of love that existed between them. Did he know too about that oath that was between David and his father respecting his father's seed? If not, I am quite sure David told him about it. The result was that Mephibosheth put away his fear and received with gratitude and assurance the proffered kindness. He could even refer to himself as 'such a dead dog as I am' and know it would not make any difference, for David was dealing with him not because of what he was in himself, but only because of the worth of the name of Jonathan to David.

As we contemplate the kindness being shown to Mephibosheth for Jonathan's sake and the worth of another being made the ground of his acceptance by David, we cannot but hear the distant chimes of a gospel that was yet to come. 'I write unto you, little children, because your sins are forgiven you for his name's sake' (1 John 2:12), that is, for the sake of the name of Jesus. Though we have up to this point been taking David rather than Jonathan to be a picture of Jesus Christ, the principle is the same—the worthless one being received in the merits of the worthy one. This certainly is the manner of our salvation by God—the grace of God comes to us for Jesus' sake.

> I stand upon His merits,
> I know no other stand,
> Not e'en where glory dwelleth
> In Emmanuel's land.

So for the moment we will switch the typology and make that covenant between David and Jonathan an illustration of the eternal covenant between the Father and the Son regarding the security of all those who believe on the Son.

Let us look more closely at that covenant made that day when it was clear that David must finally leave the court and take up the life of a wandering exile. It was made at Jonathan's insistence in the first place, but David ratified it with a solemn oath. Said Jonathan:

And thou shalt not only while I yet live show me the kindness of the LORD, that I die not: but also thou shalt not cut off thy kindness from my house for ever: no, not when the LORD hath cut off the enemies of David every one from the face of the earth. So Jonathan made a covenant with the house of David, saying, Let the LORD even require it at the hand of David's enemies. And Jonathan caused David to swear again, because he loved him: for he loved him as he loved his own soul. (1 Samuel 20:14–17)

The covenant was in two parts. First it related to Jonathan's personal survival when David should be king. Jonathan knew that to be inevitable and he was happy for it, but he wanted to be assured that David would extend to him 'the kindness of the LORD', that he die not—that is, that he would not be dealt with as a rival pretender. (By the way, there is that same phrase again, 'that you show me the kindness of the Lord'—that you be kind to me as God is kind, gracious as God is gracious.) Of course, their mutual love made anything else unthinkable, and the oath was readily given. Jonathan's other and more urgent concern was his seed, that not only would he himself enjoy this kindness while he yet lived, but also that David would not cut it off from his house for ever, not even when every one of David's foes should be cut off. Because of their love, that aspect of the covenant was sworn too. It was, then, a love-based covenant; first the love of David for Jonathan, and then that love extended to include all Jonathan's seed. And years later Mephibosheth owed his very life and any prosperity he enjoyed to that covenant, and to that alone.

Our acceptance by God is grounded also on a love-based covenant: not of our love for Him—our love always breaks down—nor even of His love for us, but on the Father's love for the Son. Jesus spoke in several places of the love of the Father for Himself; it is part of the covenant that holds the Trinity together. 'The Father loveth the Son, and hath given all things into his hand' (John 3:35). 'For the Father loveth the Son, and showeth him all things that himself doeth' (John 5:20). 'Therefore doth my Father love me, because I lay down my life...' (John 10:17).

But that love of the Father for the Son is extended to include all those who are linked by faith with the Son, 'that the love wherewith thou hast loved me may be in them...' (John 17:26). 'For the Father himself loveth you...' (John 16:27). It is a covenant that is supremely concerned with the seed of the Son, for He is certainly to have a seed. At one time it did not look as if He would. Isaiah 53 says (verse 8), 'and who shall declare his generation? for he was cut off out of the land of the living.' Cut off without a generation, having none to continue His Name—this was always a reproach in the eyes of the Jews. But verse 10 of the same chapter says, 'when thou shalt make His soul an offering for sin, *he shall see his seed.*' He is to have a seed after all!

Time and again Jesus speaks of them as those whom the Father has given Him (John 6:37, 39; 17:6, 12, 24). And this covenant is above all else about that seed.

Putting various Scriptures together, the covenant declares that a vast unspecified number of the sons of Adam have been given by the Father to the Son, that the Son has been ordained to make propitiation for human sin, and for the sake of what the Son has done the Father pledges Himself to accept all those that believe in Him. And the Father keeps that covenant made with the Son, no matter how crippled the recipients may be, and heaps benefits upon those who could be accounted His enemies. Such as is the love of the Father to the Son, so is His love to all the Son's seed.

> Dear, so very dear to God,
> Dearer I could not be;
> The love wherewith He loves the Son,
> Such is His love for me.

We must understand, then, that this covenant kindness of God, which as we shall see includes so much, is extended to us for Jesus' sake. This is important, because we are all prone to try to find something in ourselves, some quality or feeling, as a reason why God should bless us, and we are sad and depressed that in spite of all our efforts we cannot find it. You don't need to; He is going to bless and accept you, the cripple, for Jesus' sake. If you take your place as a cripple, no better than Mephibosheth, you are accepted without any more ado as 'complete' in Christ (Colossians 2:10), nothing lacking as to your acceptableness to God. He is not looking at your misshapen legs, but at the worth of your Jonathan and of His blood, which is shed for you. But, you say, I've been such a disappointment to God since I've been saved, and I fear that one day He will change His mind with regard to me. You need to tell yourself He didn't do it in the first place for your righteousness' sake; He is not therefore going to give you up when you turn out to be exactly what He said you were. There are times when we need to preach the gospel to ourselves all over again.

Restoration

Now what was this kindness towards Mephibosheth in practical terms? First, David said, 'I will restore thee all the land of Saul thy father.' Those lands had been forfeited in the fall of Saul, but David was going to restore them all to Mephibosheth for Jonathan's sake, and a man without land or property was going to become wealthy again.

This is what grace does for the penitent; it restores to him all that has been lost by his sin. Jesus not only forgives our sin, but makes good the losses we have involved ourselves in by our wrongdoing.

And how much have we not forfeited in our relationship with God, in our relations with others, and in all sorts of other situations? Our joy and peace in the Lord has been marred by sin, and that is a loss indeed. Because of the hurt we have inflicted on others, they have turned against us and even hate us. What a loss it is when those who were our friends are such no longer! Then we find ourselves in other situations of confusion and difficulty, of which we have been the cause, or at least contributor.

But when we humble ourselves to confess that we are the ones who have been wrong, Jesus proceeds to restore all such losses, or overrule them for greater good. Restoring what we have lost is the work in which He excels, the realm in which He is expert. He knows how to dry our tears and make good those losses. Our relationship with God is restored by the value of His blood, which as our Advocate He presents before God. At His touch relationships with others are healed and become even stronger than they were before, and love for one another replaces coldness. And as for the varied situations which have become marred, the heavenly Potter makes each again another vessel as seems good to the Potter to make it. And often He does so on such a scale that more seems to be restored than was lost in the first place. This is grace indeed.

> In Him the tribes of Adam boast
> More blessings than their father lost.

At the king's table

However, David promised more than the restoration of the lands of Saul; he went on to say, 'and thou shalt eat bread at my table continually,' as one of the king's sons. Thereafter Mephibosheth sat every day at that table among David's sons as if he were one himself. What a privilege! When important people came, such as foreign ambassadors, and expressed surprise to see that cripple sitting there and accorded such respect, they would be told that he was the last of the rival house, and that he was there for Jonathan's sake, and that because of the love David had for Jonathan, his place was secure.

And that is the privilege that is accorded to us cripples —we are sat at the table of grace every day as one of the King's sons. The apostle John could not get over the privilege of sitting there, and being counted as one of those sons: 'Behold, what manner of love the Father hath bestowed upon us, that we should be called the sons of God' (1 John 3:1). We are members of the rival house of Adam, and yet for Jesus' sake we are given this honoured place at the King's table.

But there was more than privilege here; there was provision. Mephibosheth was at that table as a continual guest, and as such he did not have to provide for himself. Since David was his host, David did the providing. Now that he had his own lands again he could presumably have eaten by himself in his own house and done his own providing. But had that been suggested, I am sure David would have had none of it, and would have assured him, 'You are always to eat with me, and always at my expense.'

This too is what grace does for the penitent. It sits him at the King's table and the God of grace becomes the host, while he is but a guest. A guest does not expect to do the providing; that is the part of the host. And this is the new relationship with himself into which God has brought us through Jesus, a relationship where He is the host and we are but the guests. There was a time when we tried to be the host and to have Jesus as our guest. As host we endeavoured to do our best to serve Him. But it was hard work adequately to provide for such a guest, and it never worked out. Unlike Mephibosheth, we had nothing, even after conversion. Try as we would, our hearts were empty of anything to put on the table that would please Him. But when He becomes the host, it is the other way round; it is not us providing for Him, but He for us. C. H. Spurgeon once said, 'Great saints were only great receivers.' They had no holiness, nor anything else to give Him. What we see of holiness in them was something they had received progressively from Jesus as their host, and they received it as they humbly confessed they were lacking it, and that on point after point. They were not hosts providing for Jesus, but simply guests at the table of grace. 'Of his fullness have all we received, and grace for grace' (John 1:16).

So it is when we return to the Lord in this deeper way. It is not that we might be made better hosts, better able to serve Him. That would still leave us at the head of the table, and it would not be long before He would have to withdraw and leave His place empty. It is simply that, confessing our need, we should sit down at this table of grace, and expect to receive from Jesus the opposite of what we acknowledge as sin and lack.

There, then, is the story of the magnanimity of the anointed king to the house of the rejected king, when at last it was broken in defeat—and all of it because of the covenant that had been made years before between David and Jonathan.

The oath still stands

In just one further place is that covenant mentioned again, some chapters further on, and we must take a special look at it.

The story is not a familiar one and so I must outline it

quickly. Years after the events we have been looking at, there was a famine in the land for three years (2 Samuel 21:1–14). For the first two years David did not apparently think there was any spiritual significance about it, but when it continued for the third year, he began to discern the divine hand and he enquired of the Lord. Quick as a knife God's answer came: 'It is for Saul, and for his bloody house, because he slew the Gibeonites.' The Gibeonites were those people to whom Israel had given pledges in the days of Joshua that they would spare them. Having sworn by the Lord, they could not but stand to it, although it proved that these pledges had been obtained by a trick. And so they made them 'hewers of wood and drawers of water' instead of destroying them as they did the other nations who occupied the land God had given them. But years later, Saul in his zeal for Israel had broken that pledge and had slain many of them, presumably to pillage their lands. Although David had not perpetrated the crime, he was now in a position to put it right, and God expected him to do so. So he asked the Gibeonites what he should do to make an atonement. Their answer was not to have money given to them for restitution, but, to quote, 'Let seven men of [Saul's] sons be delivered unto us, and we will hang them up unto the LORD in Gibeah of Saul.'

There were not many male descendants remaining connected with Saul. There were some sons of a concubine of his and several sons of one of his married daughters— and, of course, Mephibosheth. He was perhaps an obvious choice for one of them. And for a time it looked as if Mephibosheth might yet have to die for his grandfather's sins. And then we have the word which proved to be a glorious reprieve for Mephibosheth: 'But the king spared

Mephibosheth, the son of Jonathan the son of Saul, *because of the Lord's oath that was between them*, between David and Jonathan the son of Saul.' The covenant still stood, inviolate against this latest challenge—Mephibosheth was spared, he was not included in the seven and his place of favour remained unchanged.

The whole story is a strange and gruesome one, but not without meaning for us. However, I do not tarry to speak of that, except to emphasize this one verse where the Lord's oath between David and Jonathan is mentioned. There may well be times in our experience when we fear the covenant in the blood of Jesus may be challenged by a new turn of events, a fresh disclosure of sin in ourselves, some calamitous trouble that falls upon us, or the near approach of death itself. Our faith in grace and the power of the blood of Jesus may falter. 'Does it still avail, even for me in this situation?' we ask ourselves. 'Is there yet a place at the King's table for such as I?' Be assured, the covenant still stands, the blood of Jesus still avails for sin, and grace is still grace. If David spared Mephibosheth although he was a son of Saul, just because of the Lord's oath that was between himself and Jonathan, God will most surely spare you, although you are a son of Adam, because of the greater oath between Himself and His Son.

> His oath, His covenant, and blood,
> Support me in the 'whelming flood;
> When all around my soul gives way,
> He then is all my hope and stay.

And Mephibosheth the son of Saul answered... All of my father's house were but dead men before my lord the king: yet didst thou set thy servant among them that did eat at thine own table. What right therefore have I yet to cry any more unto the king?

2 Samuel 19:28

7

'What Right have I?... Let Him Take All'

It may well be asked at this point, does grace really work out in practical terms; does it produce positive results? Inasmuch as it seems that the chief object of the grace of God is the sinner and the failing saint, and its main work the restoration of such whenever sin and failure come in, it might be thought that man is left always failing and that the experience of restoring grace does not lead to positive holiness. Surely, some might say, the stern admonitions of the law of God should be mixed in with the message of grace to spur a man to greater heights in the future. But such a ministry does not take account of the fact that man is a cripple and will never be able by himself to make those greater heights. Mephibosheth, even when seated at David's table, was still lame on both his feet. In any case, there is no need to mix law with grace to produce holiness, for the grace of God by its power alone produces holiness in a way that the message of law never does. Grace provokes love for the One Who has bestowed it, and love in turn begets hatred of sin, self-surrender, untiring service and altogether new attitudes to others.

I cannot work my soul to save,
For that my Lord has done,
But I would work like any slave
For love of God's dear Son.

Among the many people I have known who have
responded to the fuller message of grace and see themselves
as Mephibosheths, I have observed the most obvious and
beautiful growth in holiness as they have gone on with the
Lord in this way. They themselves are largely oblivious
of this—true holiness is ever unconscious of itself—but
I can say that I have seen holiness literally walking about
on two legs and have marvelled.

The difference that the message of grace makes in a
man's life is demonstrated in this story of Mephibosheth
and David. It does not end with 2 Samuel 9, the chapter we
have been looking at. There is a sequel to it ten chapters
later. Here we see that the experience of David's grace
towards him had so captured Mephibosheth that it quite
changed his attitude, not only to David, but also to another
who had deeply wronged him, by whose action he was in
danger of losing all his lands again. It is in situations like
this that the holiness which grace produces is really seen,
and we can judge the extent to which we know the grace
of God in truth.

We must recount the incidents that led up to this real life
situation in which Mephibosheth was involved, as here
again not all readers may be familiar with them. David had
to experience for a second time what it was to be a fugitive.
The first time was as a result of Saul's persecution of him;
the second was because of the rebellion of his own son
Absalom, who by his subtlety had 'stolen the hearts of the

men of Israel.' The result was that David had to flee the
city with a few hundred faithful men. If his experiences
at the hand of Saul were painful, these at the hand of his
own son were even more so. As he fled the city, various
individuals joined his company and demonstrated their
support for him in practical ways. One of these was Ziba,
a one-time servant of Saul whom David had designated
with his family to be servants to Mephibosheth. He came
with asses loaded with foodstuff for David and his men
(2 Samuel 16). When asked where was Mephibosheth,
he told a wicked lie: 'Behold: he abideth at Jerusalem:
for he said, Today shall the house of Israel restore me the
kingdom of my father.' Actually, nothing was further from
the truth. So loyal was Mephibosheth to David, that he
neither dressed his crippled feet, nor trimmed his beard,
nor washed his clothes, all the time David was away, so
deeply did he mourn the loss of his king. The thought of
taking advantage of the situation to revive the old claim
of the house of Saul never entered his head. But as it was
politically conceivable, David believed the lie and in
disappointment and anger he made over to Ziba all the
lands which were Mephibosheth's—which was just what
Ziba was after.

We pass over that part of the story which tells of Absalom
being slain in battle and David being called by the tribes
to return to Jerusalem. As he passed over Jordan various
personages came down to meet him, Mephibosheth among
them. He came, just as he was, in his dishevelled state
of mourning. In reply to David's question, 'Wherefore
wentest thou not with me, Mephibosheth?' he replied in
words which I quote in full because they are important for
the subject we are considering:

My Lord, O king, my servant deceived me: for thy servant said, I will saddle me an ass, that I may ride thereon, and go to the king; because thy servant is lame. And he hath slandered thy servant unto my lord the king; but my lord the king is as an angel of God: do therefore what is good in thine eyes. For all of my father's house were but dead men before my lord the king: yet didst thou set thy servant among them that did eat at thine own table. What right therefore have I yet to cry any more unto the king? (2 Samuel 19:26–28)

What right have I?

Look closely at these words. He began by simply stating the facts of the situation. Ziba had deceived him. Mephibosheth had intended going to David and had ordered his ass to be saddled that he might do so. But instead, Ziba took the only two available asses for his base scheme to ingratiate himself with David and had left the crippled Mephibosheth without any means of transport. Then Ziba had slandered him, saying that he now had political intentions against David. The obvious marks of mourning Mephibosheth bore on his person were clear evidence that this was a lie. He said all this not primarily to clear himself, and certainly not to vilify Ziba, but simply because he felt he owed it to David to know that there was one heart among those who remained in Jerusalem which had loved him without wavering. Having said that, he said no more in self-defence, but left it with David to do whatever he thought right.

Then he went on to explain why he would say or ask no more, and it is here we see the extent to which grace had captured his heart. First, he said, all his father's house were but dead men before David. That is, by rights they should have been killed. Then, secondly, he acknowledged that by the magnanimity of David he had been spared and given what he did not deserve: 'yet didst thou set thy servant among them that did eat at thine own table.' He could never forget that he had been made the object of an extraordinary grace. From these two facts he draws the great conclusion that this grace had robbed him of all right to ask for anything further. 'What right therefore have I yet to cry any more unto the king?' He could never more stand up for his rights, for by right he should have been a dead man.

What sweetness there is in these words, 'What right, have I....' It is ever the effect of an experience of the undeserved grace of God. By rights we should all have been condemned and sent to hell for our sins. This is all the house of Adam deserves. But the grace of God extended to us for Jesus' sake has redeemed us from sin and given us a place at the king's table as one of His favoured sons. How can we then talk about our rights? The grace of God has robbed us forever of them all. Sitting at the king's table by grace alone, we have no right to anything else. There is a negative side to grace as well as a positive.

But we forget all this. We feel hurt and resentful and talk about our rights, and go to all sorts of lengths to stand up for them. And the only result is that we compound the troubled relations between us and others. That was the situation that existed at Philippi, as is evident from various allusions in Paul's letter to the Christians there. Relations among some of them were so unhappy that it might be doubted whether there existed at all such things as 'consolation in Christ, comfort of love, fellowship of the Spirit, tender mercies and compassions.' And he has to write that if indeed there be such things in Christ, 'fulfil ye my joy, that ye be likeminded, having the same love, being of one accord, of one mind (Philippians 2:1–2). Their lack of these sweet qualities was due to one thing: each insisting on his own rights—a far cry from Mephibosheth's attitude, 'What right have I?'

This is the reason why we need a new experience of grace of the Mephibosheth order. The experience of grace we received way back when we were first converted does not always seem vivid enough in our minds to change present attitudes. But a new conviction of sin, and a new confession of our failure leading to a new experience of God's forgiveness and restoration should, if we let God go deep enough, surely lead us to say, 'What right have I therefore?' with regard to the practical issues that now confront us.

Let him take all

The grace that Mephibosheth had received from David had yet a further effect on him, as comes out in the next incident. David realized that he had been misled with regard to him, and he found himself in the embarrassing situation of having made over all his lands to Ziba. And Ziba was standing right there welcoming him back with the others. He could not easily rescind that order, as Ziba had without doubt rendered valuable service in bringing him the provisions he had. So David said, 'Thou and Ziba divide the land.' To this Mephibosheth replied in words of sublime nobility: 'Let him take all, forasmuch as my lord the king is come again in peace unto his own house'

(2 Samuel 19:30). The grace of David towards him in the past had begotten such a love for David himself, that personal considerations mattered nothing to him, now that he had got his king back again.

So for us. A true experience of the grace of God through Christ always attaches the recipient to the person of the Giver, so much so that he is prepared to yield up personal considerations in the joy of having the Lord back again after, say, a period of alienation. So great is his satisfaction in restored fellowship with the One that grace has attached him to, that he has no stomach to continue the contention with another over rights and disputed points; and he says in effect what Mephibosheth said: 'Yea, let him take all, forasmuch as my lord the king is come again in peace unto his own house.' If this is not holiness, what is? And it is simply the product of an experience of grace, something the law could never produce.

As an illustration of this I remember a lady telling me about her son and daughter-in-law who had recently left England to take up a business appointment in East Africa. At the time of leaving they were involved in a dispute over their share in a will or something similar, a dispute which was likely to lead to litigation. They left strict instructions that mother was to continue the battle on their behalf. Out in East Africa they came in touch with some vital Christians and through them they themselves found Jesus Christ as their personal Saviour and Lord. The lady told me that all their letters to her were now full of their new-found experience of joy in Christ; there was no mention in them at all of the dispute and the points at issue. She was at a loss to understand their unconcern for what had once so agitated them—until later she herself came to know the Lord! The attitude of that young couple was in effect Mephibosheth's: 'Yea, let him take all, forasmuch as my lord the king is come again in peace.'

Such an attitude is a very compelling witness in the eyes of the world, whereas the reverse makes us odious indeed to them. While we are not experiencing the grace of God and are cold and self-righteous, our attitude will invariably be that of the man who came to Jesus saying, 'Master, speak to my brother, that he divide the inheritance with me.' Apparently the point at issue was the old one of an inheritance—a will again—and he wanted to enlist the Lord on his side. He only received the abrupt reply, 'Man, who made me a judge or a divider over you?' (Luke 12:13–14). How little Jesus can mean to us if that is our attitude. Happy the man who has so come to love the Lord and see his riches in Him that he can truly sing the hymn:

Take the whole world, but give me Jesus.

All this then is a by-product of the message of grace.

It must be said, however, that this sort of response to the grace of God does not happen easily or automatically. 'just like that.' So often our first reactions are the wrong ones. The old Adam within us rears itself up and asks for its rights, and is not willing in the least for the other to take all—until the Lord deals with us and we repent. Then Jesus brings us back to the old place of peace: 'What right have I... let him take all.' This means that when at last we do adopt this gracious attitude it is no thanks to us; it has come as a result of God's forgiveness and cleansing at the foot of the cross of Jesus.

God's great gamble

So it is that grace, the unconditional love of God, does indeed produce holiness in those who are its beneficiaries. If God had tightened up on grace, and inserted extra, more stringent conditions lest men abuse it, it might presumably seem to have given careless ones the challenge they needed but it would have made others despair. Those extra conditions would have been the death of them, for they might not have been able to fulfil them, and then where would they have been? God therefore decided to take a calculated risk in dealing with men wholly on the grounds of grace. If that doesn't turn men round and motivate them for real holiness, He has no other way. But God's great gamble has paid off, as the transformed lives of myriads of the redeemed will testify. Or has it, in your case?

And I am this day tender, though anointed king; and these men the sons of Zeruiah be too hard for me.

2 Samuel 3.39

8

'Tender Though Anointed King'

For the greater part of his life David had to contend
with two problems. They were his two captains, Joab
and his brother Abishai, the sons of Zeruiah, who were
ostensibly the most devoted of all his servants—but they
were too hard for him. We shall briefly survey their story,
and I imagine its application to ourselves will be only too
obvious. In contrast to them David's true character will be
seen to stand out in extraordinary beauty. So we will get
yet another sight of Jesus.

'And I am this day tender, though anointed king and
these men the sons of Zeruiah be too hard for me.' With
these words David dissociated himself from an action of
Joab in which he thought he was doing David service. He
had killed Abner, the captain of the opposing forces of the
house of Saul, just as he was negotiating with David to
bring all Israel over to David's side. Joab could not understand him, dealing so gently with his enemies—giving
Abner and his deputation a feast and sending them away
in peace. And so he did what he thought ought to be done
in such a case, On some pretext he called Abner back
to Hebron, and drawing him aside as if he would speak
peacefully to him, 'smote him there under the fifth rib',
only to find that his action caused no satisfaction to David

at all, but only deep, deep grief. David expressed that grief in the most open manner, weeping aloud at the grave of Abner and refusing to eat till the sun went down, so that all the people 'understood that day it was not of the king to slay Abner.' He said to his servants, 'The Lord shall reward the doer of evil according to his wickedness.'

Joab too hard for David

And this deed was done by one of the most devoted of David's servants, one who had been with him from the beginning, sharing his travail as well as his triumph, and who seemed to love him with such fierce devotion that he would do anything for him. But as David said, he was too hard for him. Years later, after the rebellion and fall of Absalom, Joab basely slew Amasa, Absalom's captain, just as he too was changing over to David's side. On these two occasions Joab 'shed the blood of war in peace,' as David himself put it (1 Kings 2:5). 'But they were David's enemies,' Joab might have said in justification. Yes, but as a result of David's gentle diplomacy they were in process of becoming his friends—but Joab spoilt it all.

This hardness was not only found in Joab; it was equally in his brother Abishai. It was he who would have slain Saul as he lay asleep at David's feet that night in the camp, had not David restrained him. And it was he who asked that he might take Shimei's head off when he cursed David as he fled from Absalom, to which David replied, 'What have I to do with you, ye sons of Zeruiah? so let him curse, because the Lord hath said unto him, Curse David' (2 Samuel 16:10). And there are yet other instances that could be quoted.

In so reproving the sons of Zeruiah and dissociating himself from their actions and attitudes, he revealed his true character for all to see—tender though anointed king. 'And all the people took notice of it, and it pleased them,' we read in 2 Samuel 3:36. They liked a king like that.

Tender-hearted David

If we can give a list of instances where the sons of Zeruiah were too hard for David, we can also give numbers of instances where David was seen to be 'tender though anointed king.' He demonstrated this trait even before he was made king in his whole attitude to Saul, always refusing to lift up his hand against him. Then, when ultimately the news came that Saul and his son had fallen in battle, he greeted it with sorrow rather than with joy, even though it cleared his way to the throne, and uttered a moving lament over his old king and enemy—one of the most beautiful chapters in the Bible (2 Samuel 1). 'Saul and Jonathan were lovely and pleasant in their lives.' We can understand him saying that of Jonathan, but he said it also of Saul, demonstrating how much he loved and even appreciated him, although he had suffered so much at his hands. What manner of man is this!

And then he took up the same attitude to Abner, whose murder at the hand of Joab we have just considered. We must remember that Abner had been Saul's captain and had been associated with Saul's persecution of David. It was Saul *and Abner* who had hunted David 'as a partridge in the mountains.' And yet David mourned publicly for him, saying, 'Know ye not that there is a prince and a great man fallen this day in Israel?' (2 Samuel 3:38).

We see him yet again 'tender though anointed king' with regard to Absalom, that son of his who had led the nation against him, causing him and his few hundred followers to flee the city. David had no option but to send his small army against him (2 Samuel 18), though he was careful to instruct his captains, 'Deal gently for my sake with the young man, even with Absalom.' But when Joab did not do that at all, but rather thrust him through with a spear as he hung suspended from a tree, David broke his heart and mourned for him in words that have become famous for their gentle pathos: 'O my son Absalom, my son, my son Absalom! would God I had died for thee, O Absalom, my son, my son!'

In these instances and in others which I do not mention now, we see him 'tender though anointed king.'

The lamb in the midst of the throne

Here David is a picture of the Lord Jesus, if ever he is, 'tender though anointed king.' This was in effect what the apostle John saw in Revelation 4 and 5. Having seen in chapter 4 'a throne set in heaven' and 'one sat upon it,' he is given in chapter 5 a second look at that throne as we read (verse 6), 'I beheld, and, lo, in the midst of the throne... stood a lamb.' It is Jesus anointed King, co-partner of the Father's royal throne, exercising all its authority, but doing so as the Lamb. Thereafter that throne is spoken of as 'the throne of God and of the Lamb' (22:1, 3). Now a lamb is the gentlest of God's creatures. You can do what you will with a lamb, and it will not turn and rend you like other beasts of the jungle—fit picture of the Lord Jesus, the 'meek and lowly in heart.' And in this phrase, 'the Lamb in the midst of the throne,' we see Him Who humbled Himself so low, exalted to the highest throne to rule the world—but still 'tender though anointed King.'

This gives character to that throne and conditions its commands binding on us, and shows as wherein we have turned aside, and wherein we must return. There is nothing so searching as the vision of Jesus as 'the Lamb in the midst of the throne,' for by nature that is not our disposition at all.

In our zeal too hard for him

In the light of this we can see that Jesus still has among his disciples today the sons of Zeruiah who in their fancied zeal are too hard for Him, and from whose actions and attitudes He has so often to dissociate Himself, did they but know it. Their hardness is seen in the way they act and react to others, resenting them when they are hurt by them, criticizing them when they appear to be wrong in their behaviour or their doctrinal views. Especially is this seen when the point at issue has to do with the work of the Lord in one way or another. If there is a fault in another in that sphere, we seem to think that that excuses everything we may say or do, and that we have a perfect right to take a holiday off from love and 'go into bat' just as we feel disposed. In those situations we can be plain rude and unkind to one another and speak to those we disagree with in a way the world would hardly do, and yet think we do Jesus service in the matter. Nothing, repeat nothing, excuses lack of love. True, we must sometimes 'earnestly contend for the faith which was once delivered unto the saints' (Jude 3). But remember Jesus is tender though anointed

King. It may be that after you have had your say and made
your point He has to turn away from you, saying, 'What
have I to do with you, ye sons of Zeruiah? Ye be too hard
for me.'

The great hymn writer, Faber, seemed to include
himself as such a one when he wrote his hymn *Souls of
Men*. Having given us the verse:

> For the love of God is broader
> Than the measures of man's mind;
> And the heart of the Eternal
> Is most wonderfully kind,

he then has to add, almost with a sob, the next verse:

> But we make His love too narrow,
> By false limits of our own,
> And we magnify His strictness
> With a zeal He would not own.

He seems to imply that he has not demonstrated that
love, that kindness in his life as he should, and that he, and
we, have been too hard for Him.

Carnal zeal

We must look more closely at the fierce loyalty of
the sons of Zeruiah to David that caused him so much
grief over the years. Did you know that Zeruiah was
their mother, not their father, and that she was David's
sister? In the Old Testament men are usually named as the
sons of their father, but David always refers to Joab and
Abishai as the sons of their mother. He knew her well, of

course, and perhaps he called them so because he saw the traits of a strong, over-bearing woman coming out in her sons. Perhaps David used to shake his head sadly over them and say, 'They are true sons of their mother.' Their fierce devotion is a picture of that carnal zeal among us Christians that causes not only similar grief to Jesus, but contention and hurt among the saints.

It was what it was for two reasons. First, in Joab's case it arose out of ignorance of David's true character. Joab was a graceless man himself and he could never understand grace in David. Again and again David baffled him; he reacted to people and circumstances in a way that Joab never would have done. This comes out when David is so overcome with grief over the death of his rebel son Absalom 'that the victory that day was turned into mourning.' Joab took him to task and said, 'Thou hast shamed this day the faces of all thy servants... in that thou lovest thine enemies and hatest thy friends.' No, Joab, it is not true that he hates his friends, but he certainly loves his enemies, especially this one. Just because there was no correspondence in Joab's heart with this sort of quality, he could not but misunderstand David, and his activity would so often be at variance with David's spirit.

And so for us too; we do not see that there is a Lamb in the midst of the throne. It can only be that we think there is a lion or a tiger in the midst of the throne, judging by the way we act and react and yet feel no conviction of sin, even thinking we do God service. What we do in actual fact is subconsciously to assume that He is altogether such a one as ourselves. And inasmuch as we have more of the disposition of the lion or the tiger than of anything else, and inasmuch as we assume He feels much the same about people as we do, we think it is quite permissible for us to act that way towards them too, and even to do so in His Name. That is precisely what Psalm 50 charges us with in a most penetrating verse (verse 21): 'These things hast thou done, and I kept silence; thou thoughtest that I was altogether such an one as thyself: but I will reprove thee, and set them in order before thine eyes.'

Selfish considerations

There was, moreover, another element in Joab's apparent zeal for David—the element of selfish considerations. Deep down Joab was motivated by concern for his own position as captain of the host. If Abner had indeed changed to David's side and brought all Israel with him, where would that put Joab? Two dominant leaders in the same army would hardly do. Well, Joab's sword settled that one all right. Then there was a little (!) matter of personal revenge to be settled too. Abner had reluctantly slain Asahel, the younger brother of Joab and Abishai, in a previous battle; Asahel would not call off his relentless chase of Abner, and Abner had no alternative but to give him a backward lunge with his spear as he ran, which proved fatal. Joab's slaying of Abner settled that score too. But, unlike Abner's killing of Asahel, this was a clear case of 'shedding the blood of war in peace'—indeed, David had just concluded a peace treaty with him. And yet Joab professed to David he was concerned just for the cause and asserted that Abner had come as a spy. But the real motives were these personal considerations, as they were in some other instances that could be quoted.

Oh these mixed motives in our apparent zeal and service

for Jesus—witness the contentions that sometimes rend our churches! What we do of service is not only done for the Lord, but for ourselves as well. We are as jealous for our own position as Joab was for his. And even the settling of an old score, the desire to get even with another, can come into it. I believe it is true to say that the flesh in the service of God, even at its best, is an abomination to Him.

Little wonder, then, that David, the one who was tender though anointed king, should dissociate himself from these violent sons of Zeruiah. But David did more than this; after the death of Abner he pronounced upon them an anathema, quite astonishing in its vehemence (2 Samuel 3:29): 'Let there not fail from the house of Joab one that hath an issue, or that is a leper, or that leaneth on a staff, or that falleth on the sword, or that lacketh bread!' Could a man say more? I do not criticize David for saying this; I'm glad he did; it could not then be said he connived at what they had done, although he had to continue with them, for he had no way just then of getting rid of them. Later, on his death bed, he gave instructions to Solomon with regard to Joab 'Let not his hoar head go down to the grave in peace' (1 Kings 2:6).

The wrath of the Lamb

This is what we may call 'the wrath of the Lamb,' a phrase we get in the book of Revelation (6:16). It was no denial of his gentleness, but rather an expression of it. It was because he was tender though anointed king that he could not but pass judgment on one who had been anything but this. How else could he hold up his face to the widows of Abner and Amasa and their children, who in each case had lost husband and father? It was his very compassion for them that led him to advise Solomon with regard to Joab as he did. It is so with the Lord Jesus. It is because He is the Lamb in the midst of the throne that His wrath falls on those who have violated the principles of the Lamb to the hurt and sorrow of others. It is just because as the Lamb He loves the poor and needy that He cannot but judge those that oppress them.

This is, of course, one of the principles on which the unbelieving world will be judged, and on which He will one day bring down all oppressive regimes. But it also applies in a rather different way to the believer. He, too, may become subject to the 'wrath of the Lamb', although this is not in order that he should be punished for his sins. That was finished for ever at Calvary. In his case it is a disciplinary chastening to provoke him to repentance and to restore him to fellowship with the Lamb.

Actually Joab sealed his own fate. Although he did not turn aside after Absalom but remained loyal to David throughout that rebellion, he did turn aside after Adonijah, who tried vainly to set himself up to succeed David in Solomon's place. That is another story which you can read for yourself in 1 Kings 2. Suffice it to say that Joab found himself supporting the wrong cause, for Solomon was immediately crowned king. And although Joab fled to the tabernacle of the Lord for refuge, Solomon had him killed nonetheless.

The carnal Christian who will not repent will inevitably take a false step and end quite discredited. God is not mocked.

When the Spirit brings revival....

When the Holy Spirit brings renewal to a church or a group He almost invariably begins with us sons of Zeruiah, though we may never have seen ourselves as such before. But He reproves us and sets things in order before our eyes, and we see He is quite other than ourselves. We see He is the Lamb in the midst of the throne and we have been anything but lambs. And as the Spirit works repentance and people share what God has shown them, others in turn see Jesus as He really is and they are convicted too. The picture of the Lamb in the midst of the throne becomes ever clearer in the light of what people share He is showing them, and the Spirit moves from life to life and further matters of sin are revealed.

One of the ways, then, in which the vision of Jesus is given is by the nature of the very things He convicts the saints of. In this way we see His outline as it really is, tender though anointed King. You can pick up accounts of God's working in revival almost at random, and see this is the way of the Spirit's working. I recently came across a book about the Wycliffe Bible Translators, in one chapter of which is told the story of how renewal came to one of their base camps in South America:

Jerry told me about an evening communion service held sometime after the air crash. They didn't get around to serving the bread and wine until after midnight. It seemed that everybody on base—more than four hundred—had something to confess and wanted to do it publicly. Men, women and children rose to their feet, tearfully confessing such things as pride, selfishness, haughtiness, intolerance, envy and resentment. On into the night the service went until the people of God got right with God—and their neighbours.

Yes, that is so often the way the Holy Spirit works, from person to person, from one thing to another, from the obvious and more blatant sins to the more subtle matters of motives, as we see Him tender though anointed King.

I once heard of how a student in a Bible school, at a time when the Holy Spirit was working, confessed that he had been convicted of selfishness. When a parcel of goodies came from home, he would not open it until he got to the privacy of his room. There he could eat the contents alone, without feeling he should share them with others. And now he was asking forgiveness of his fellows. What was this that was going on? Was it a game they were playing? Was this an orgy of confession, or a formula for renewal they had adopted? Nothing of the sort! As one or two began to share what God had shown them, they all began to see Jesus as He really was, that He was the Lamb in the midst of the throne, and they began to see where they had been too hard for Him, too selfish for Him. Soon it seemed that everybody was under conviction of sin, if not about one thing, then another, and many were released by Jesus and led into joy and new love for one another.

The sons of Zebedee

Before we close this chapter I must ask you to note that Jesus in the days of His flesh had among His disciples two sons of Zeruiah who were too hard for Him—only they were called the sons of Zebedee, James and John. Jesus aptly surnamed them (or should we say, nicknamed them) 'Boanerges' which is, 'the sons of thunder' (Mark 3:17). In view of the fact that John is always known now as 'the apostle of love,' it is difficult to believe he was not always that way. Indeed, as we find him in his early days, he was an exact replica of Joab. On at least three occasions Jesus had to say virtually the same words as David of old, 'What have I to do with you, ye sons of Zebedee? These men, the sons of Zebedee, be too hard for Me.' The first occasion was when James and John came to Jesus with a special request, put up to it by their mother. 'Grant unto us that we may sit, one on thy right hand, and the other on thy left hand, in thy glory' (Mark 10:37). We must admire their certainty that Jesus was the Messiah and was coming into His kingdom. What was not so admirable was that they wanted to book the two top places for themselves, ahead of the others, and they attempted to get their request in before them. There is the motive of selfish consideration for you, if ever there was a case, and the others did not appreciate it, for they would have liked those two places themselves. It was plain self-seeking on both sides. Lovingly Jesus rebuked them: 'Ye know not what ye ask... [it] is not mine to give.'

The second was when John said, 'Master, we saw one casting out demons in thy name; and we forbade him, because he followeth not with us' (Luke 9:49); John thought he had done right, that he had been orthodox and had stood up for orthodoxy. Granted, this man was following, but he was not following *with us*; he did not belong to our clique, did not put the message our way. So we forbade him to do it and did our best to get him to desist. This was plainly the sin of intolerance. The apostle of love? Not much love about that! Here, too, Jesus challenged him: 'Forbid him not: for he that is not against us is for us.'

The third occasion was when on the way to Jerusalem a Samaritan village would not receive them and, presumably, refused to provide any hospitality for the night. At that James and John were greatly incensed and said, 'LORD, wilt thou that we command fire to come down from heaven, and consume them, even as Elijah did?' (Luke 9:54). How dare they treat us like that! And they remembered how Elijah once acted, and they wanted to have them consumed. Here they were definitely living up to their name of 'sons of thunder.' Quite plainly we have here the sin of vindictiveness, and that in the Lord's service. His word of reproof to them was even stronger than before. 'Ye know not what manner of spirit ye are of.' 'What spirit, Lord?' they might have said. I know He would have replied, 'The devil; what you have just said is of the devil.'

We can sum up these three expressions of the flesh in the sons of Zebedee this way: as regards their brethren there was a desire to excel; as regards those that did not follow with them, the desire to forbid; and as regards those that opposed them, the desire to consume. From all these three Jesus utterly dissociated Himself. The greater than David said, 'What have I to do with you, ye sons of Zebedee. I am this day tender, though anointed King.'

Son of thunder—Apostle of love

However, there is a word of encouragement for us here. This John, this son of thunder, this carnal Christian, this man so like Joab, ultimately became so different that he has come to be known as 'the apostle of love.' In his epistles his message reiterated again and again was, 'Little children, love one another, as He hath loved you.' The change really happened to him, but I am sure not without many repentances before the Lord. Indeed, I imagine he responded to each of those three challenges the Lord spoke to him by humble confession: 'Thou are right and I am wrong.' Did he weep on the Lord's shoulder as he did so? Anyway, we know he certainly leaned on Jesus' bosom at that last supper, forgiven and restored. And as he went on with the Lord, often coming with his lack of love and much else, grace progressively put into him what he confessed was not there naturally.

Too hard for Him? There is a sense in which we are not too hard for Him. He can change even us, if we go the way of repentance that we have suggested John went, and if we look to Jesus to fill our confessed emptiness with His fullness.

Behold, a son shall be born to thee, who shall be a man of rest; and I will give him rest from all his enemies round about: for his name shall be Solomon [that is, Peaceable], *and I will give peace and quietness unto Israel in his days.*

1 Chronicles 22:9

He shall have dominion also from sea to sea, and from the River unto the ends of the earth....
Yea, all kings shall fall down before him: all nations shall serve him....
His name shall endure for ever: his name shall be continued as long as the sun....

Psalm 72:8, 11, 17

The queen of the south... came from the uttermost parts of the earth to hear the wisdom of Solomon; and, behold, a greater than Solomon is here.

Matthew 12:42

9

Solomon in All His Glory

We have now covered the stories of David and Saul, David and Jonathan, David and Mephibosheth and David and Joab, with all their rich teaching and application for our lives. In order to confine myself to the limits I have set for this book, I must pass over further absorbing incidents in the life of David, in all of which he is a type of Christ with equally rich teaching for us. There is the story of *David and Absalom* (2 Samuel 15), who stole the hearts of the men of Israel from his father, picturing the way in which the world and the god of this world can steal our hearts from Jesus and cause us to drive Him once again from His throne. When that happens with all its unhappy results, we may well ask ourselves the question the tribes of Israel ultimately asked themselves, 'Now therefore why speak ye not a word of bringing the king back?' (2 Samuel 19:10).

There is also the story of *David and Adonijah* (1 Kings 1), that other son of his who tried to pre-empt David's coronation of Solomon as his successor, and who 'exalted himself saying, I will be king.' We too could be among those who 'love to have the preeminence' (3 John 9), and would set ourselves up as kings among God's people. Adonijah had to realize that his project of self-aggrandizement was

doomed, and he fled for refuge and 'caught hold of the
horns of the altar.' We also may flee and 'cling to the old
rugged cross,' when such sin is finding us out.

David not complete without Solomon

All these I must pass by as outside my present scope. But
there is one part of the story I must not pass over; it is that
of *David and Solomon*. David's career without Solomon
would not be complete. David himself knew it in his old
age. Although many things had reached a glorious climax
for him, not all his hopes had been fulfilled. He was not
to be permitted to build the temple of the Lord, on which
he had so set his heart. The borders of his country, though
greatly extended, had not been enlarged as much as he had
hoped, nor as much as they needed to be to ensure Israel's
security. Then, too, he had been a man of war and was not
the man of peace that Israel now needed. As many a father
has done since, he transferred his unfulfilled hopes and
dreams to his son. Only in Solomon, if he fulfilled those
dreams, would his life be complete. And so he composed
one of his noblest psalms, Psalm 72. Indeed, its final
words, 'The prayers of David the son of Jesse are ended,'
seem to suggest it was the last he ever wrote. It is entitled
'A Psalm for Solomon,' and in it he expresses his hopes
for Solomon as the completion of his own life. Indeed,
it is more than an expression of hope for Solomon; it is
given us as declared statements of what he will be and do,
prophecies of the magnificence of his kingdom and of the
compassionate justice of his rule.

Solomon a type of Christ

If David is not complete without Solomon as to his earthly career, it is certainly the case when we regard David as a type of Christ, as we have been doing. You do not get the whole picture of Jesus Christ just in David. You need Solomon in all his glory, as revealed in this psalm, to complete the picture. David is a picture of Christ in His sufferings. His exaltation to the throne of God and His present work of warring with Satan to save men. But Solomon is a type of Christ as the Prince of Peace in His millennial reign, which is yet to come. To this old earth Jesus is yet to return to be vindicated in the very place where He was put to shame. On this old earth He is yet to rule in righteousness and peace. On its soil all nations will yet serve Him. By the very nature of the case, that is man's rebelliousness, His kingdom can only be established by apocalyptic judgements; but established it will be, and the kingdoms of this world shall become the kingdoms of Jehovah and of His Christ. Under His rule all oppression will cease, ideal conditions will obtain among men and nations, and even the physical creation will be beautified as never before. It is the golden age of humanity, to which innumerable prophecies in both Old and New Testaments point forward. Revelation 20 tells us that He will thus reign for a thousand years, and those who have suffered with Him here will be associated with Him then. This is what we call the millennium, and that is why I use the phrase, 'His millennial reign.' Whether that millennium is to be taken as an exact thousand years, or a great protracted period of time, it matters not. The fact is that the greater than Solomon in all His glory is going to be the universal Lord.

A recent re-reading of the glory of Solomon's reign has left me, I must confess, almost breathless. Has there ever been a kingdom more magnificent? The extent of its borders were infinitely greater than anything Israel had known before. Solomon reigned from the Euphrates to the borders of Egypt. More than that, adjacent nations for one reason or another became tributary to him, in that they brought him regular tribute money. Yet other countries vied with one another to bring him immense voluntary gifts, coming from great distances to do so. He had peace on all sides round about him, and economic stability within his own nation: 'Israel dwelt safely, every man under his vine and under his fig tree, from Dan even to Beersheba, all the days of Solomon' (1 Kings 4:25). Riches, chariots and horsemen were brought together from all sides, so that special store cities had to be built throughout the land. As a result of his initiative and planning he saw arise in Jerusalem four great and beautiful structures: first the house of the Lord; then his own palace; following that the house of the forest of Lebanon where his throne was placed; and then the house for Pharaoh's daughter whom he had taken to wife. The scale and style of his court, 'the meat of his table, and the sitting of his servants, and the attendance of his ministers, and their apparel, and his cupbearers, and his ascent by which he went up unto the house of the LORD' were such that when the Queen of Sheba saw it all, 'there was no more spirit in her' (1 Kings 10:5). So much gold was brought in from other countries that even the drinking vessels in his palace were all made of pure gold; 'none were made of silver,' we read; 'it was nothing accounted of in the days of Solomon.' Most important and impressive of all was that, 'all the earth sought to Solomon, to hear his wisdom, which God had put in his heart.' There were always kings and philosophers from all over the world who had come to sit and listen. To sum it all up the narrative says, 'So king Solomon exceeded all the kings of the earth for riches and for wisdom.'

By comparison David's court and kingdom must have seemed, to those who remembered it, a very modest affair, quite eclipsed by Solomon's. But it was not so; it was the same kingdom—David's—but grown to completion, the fulfilment of David's dream expressed in Psalm 72.

So of the kingdom of Christ in its visible manifestation in the millennium. The glory of that kingdom might seem to quite eclipse that kingdom of His as we know it today, existing as it does only in the hearts of believers, without any visible manifestation. But it is not really so; it is the same King and the same kingdom, but come to its ultimate perfection. It needs Solomon as well as David to give the complete picture of the Lord Jesus Christ.

Those who have read carefully the book of Revelation will know, of course, that the millennium is not the end of the story. With the completion of that golden age on earth, we are told that 'the elements shall melt with fervent heat, the earth also and the works that are therein shall be burned up' (2 Peter 3:10–12) in order to give place to the new heaven and the new earth. But even so, the millennium with Christ reigning on earth is far more the subject of the prophecies of the Bible than the ultimate new heaven and new earth.

A Psalm for Solomon

It is the vision of that kingdom of Christ on earth which is the subject of Psalm 72, possibly one of the most important of all the messianic psalms. In looking at it we find that it is entitled, as I have said, 'A Psalm for Solomon.' I am aware of the fact that the Revised Standard Version translates the title *'A Psalm of Solomon'*, as if it were written by him. It seems that linguistically the Hebrew can be translated either way. The Authorized Version acknowledges this in the margin. But the fact that the psalm ends with the words 'The prayers of David the son of Jesse are ended' does seem to indicate that this is David's psalm, not Solomon's. Then the very first verse is a prayer for 'the king's son,' and this too seems to confirm the rightness of the decision of the Authorized Version to give it the title 'A Psalm for Solomon' in the body of the text.

It is possible it was composed during that short time when the aged David and Solomon reigned together. You will remember, David had Solomon anointed quickly because of the rebellion of Adonijah. Maybe it was then that the old king looked ahead and put down in this psalm all he could wish for, all he could pray for, for his son and for the rule he was to exercise. He had some time earlier laid down his dictum for kingship: 'The God of Israel said, the Rock of Israel spake to me, He that ruleth over men must be just, ruling in the fear of God' (2 Samuel 23:3). Here he amplifies it to such an extent that, wittingly or unwittingly, he is pointing beyond Solomon to Messiah Himself.

Thy judgements... Thy righteousness

The psalm begins with a short comprehensive prayer for Solomon:

Give the king thy judgments, O God, and thy righteousness unto the king's son.

This is in the nature of an introduction to the whole psalm, and an understanding of it will give us the key in which all the melody that follows is set.

In this verse we have two words, judgment and righteousness, which appear everywhere in the Old Testament prophets and are almost always coupled together. We must understand the special sense in which the Hebrew writers used them. Judgment to them was not firstly *against* someone, but judgment *on behalf* of someone. When David said in another psalm, 'Judge me, O Lord,' he did not mean, May I have a day of judgment all to myself. He meant judge on behalf of me, defend my cause, vindicate me. And therefore the word can be rendered justice, but even that is not as good as judgment, once you know what it means. The other word coupled so often with it, righteousness, is similar and means equity, that is, justice which is even-handed.

Poor and needy

Now the recipients of this judgment of God, this justice, are nearly always said in the Old Testament to be the 'poor and needy.' This phrase is littered throughout the Old Testament. Keep your eyes open for it and you will be surprised how often it occurs. It appears three times in this psalm alone. You will find that the poor and needy are usually those who are suffering oppression at the hands of others. Sometimes it is because they are poor and needy without any to help that they are oppressed; other times it is the very oppression they suffer that renders them poor and needy. The oppression has, of course, taken and still takes various forms—social, racial, religious or political. Sometimes the poor and needy suffer from one individual who dominates them. On other occasions enslavement comes to them from false rule and/authority, what we call today oppressive regimes. But you will find from the many occurrences of the phrase 'poor and needy' that Jehovah, the God of grace, is always declared to be on the side of such, and judges on their behalf, and one day when His anointed One comes again He will 'break in pieces the oppressor' (verse 4), whoever he may be.

So whereas the word begins with the meaning of judgment on *behalf* of the poor and needy, it goes on to mean judgment *against* those that oppress them, and ultimately against all wrongdoers. The latter is the way in which the New Testament and we ourselves today normally use the word, but this is the process by which it has come to have that meaning.

One other thing must be understood about this before we go further. It is that to the Old Testament prophets and psalmists the poor and needy whose oppressors Jehovah would crush were invariably seen as Israel. After all, what nation has been as wronged and oppressed as they in their long history? The prophets, then, were quite unashamedly Israel-oriented in their approach. But in proving Himself to be on the side of poor and needy Israel, He gave a revelation of what He is in Himself in any case. Israel and her needs were only the foil by which to give a dazzling display of Himself as the God of grace, which grace would be applicable not only to Israel as a nation, but to any individual whether in Israel or out of Israel who was poor, needy and oppressed and who would look to Him. This, too, is something of the process by which the New Testament message of the grace of God has developed. What an encouragement this is for us to be honest about our current position and take the place of the poor and needy, thus qualifying for the bountiful attentions of a God of grace.

Let it be laid down, then, at the beginning of this psalm that it is the blessed quality of the Godhead ever to judge on behalf of the poor and needy. This is the reason why the opening prayer is, 'Give the king thy judgments, O God,' i.e. may he manifest and reflect in his rule this beautiful quality of the God he represents. And that is the very thing we see Solomon, and the greater than Solomon, doing throughout this psalm.

He shall judge the poor of the people, he shall save the children of the needy, and shall break in pieces the oppressor (verse 4).

For he shall deliver the needy when he crieth; the poor also, and him that hath no helper (verse 12). He shall have pity on the poor and needy, and the souls of the needy he shall save (verse 13).

He shall redeem their souls from oppression and violence; and precious shall their blood be in his sight (verse 14).

It is because of this compassionate judgment of His on behalf of those that have no helper that it is said:

He shall come down like rain upon the mown grass: as showers that water the earth (verse 6).

Mown grass is wounded grass, and His rule will be as rain to heal the wounds of men. But the redeemed today do not have to wait till the millennium to experience this. They have already found Jesus healing their wounds, soothing their sorrows and driving away their fear.

It is because of this same compassionate justice that

All kings shall fall down before him: all nations shall serve him (verse 11).

There are two words in the Hebrew, I understand, for 'serve' or 'submit.' The one is to do so with bad grace, because you've got to; your opponent is too strong for you. The other word is to submit voluntarily. The latter is the word here; 'all nations shall serve him;' they will do it voluntarily, gladly. And the reason? The next verse tells us, 'for he shall deliver the needy when he crieth....' They want to enjoy the gracious beneficence of His rule, along with others. Not by force of arms will our Solomon extend His influence, but by the 'wisdom that is from above,' which is 'peaceable, gentle, and easy to be entreated' (James 3:17).

This is the reason too why

all nations shall call him blessed (verse 17).

They will call Him such because of the infinite benefits and happiness they have enjoyed at His hands.

So it is that grace and truth will be the foundation of His throne in the millennium, as it is the source of all His glory even now in the eyes of the redeemed.

Jesus, then, is not only our David in the present time, but our Solomon in the coming day.

The Psalm as a whole

Now let us read the psalm as a whole with the same spirit of praise to God and worship that David manifested when he first wrote it. Aged as he was, I believe it was an intense experience to him as he wrote or dictated these glorious prophecies. An old writer has divided up the psalm as follows: *A glowing description of the reign of Messiah as righteous*, verses 1–7; *as universal*, verses 8–11; *as beneficent*, verses 12–14; *as unending*, verses 15–17; to which is added *a doxology*, verses 18–19, and *a postscript*, verse 20. I gratefully follow these clear divisions.

Notice as you read it the charming dualism of Hebrew poetry. Nearly every phrase is expressed twice, the second expression slightly varying and amplifying the first— beautiful!

The reign of Messiah as righteous

Give the king thy judgments, O God, and thy righteousness unto the king's son.

He shall judge thy people with righteousness, and thy poor with judgment.

The mountains shall bring peace to the people, and the little hills, by righteousness.

He shall judge the poor of the people, he shall save the children of the needy, and shall break in pieces the oppressor.

They shall fear thee as long as the sun and moon endure, throughout all generations.

He shall come down like rain upon the mown grass: as showers that water the earth.

In his days shall the righteous flourish; and abundance of peace so long as the moon endureth.

The reign of Messiah as universal

He shall have dominion also from sea to sea, and from the River unto the ends of the earth.

They that dwell in the wilderness shall bow before him; and his enemies shall lick the dust.

The kings of Tarshish and of the isles shall bring presents: the kings of Sheba and Seba shall offer gifts.

Yea, all kings shall fall down before him: all nations shall serve him.

The reign of Messiah as beneficent

For he shall deliver the needy when he crieth; the poor also, and him that hath no helper.

He shall have pity on the poor and needy, and the souls of the needy he shall save.

He shall redeem their soul from oppression and violence and precious shall their blood be in his sight.

The reign of Messiah as unending

And he shall live, and to him shall be given of the gold of Sheba: prayer also shall be made for him continually; and daily shall he be praised.

There shall be a handful of corn in the earth upon the

top of the mountains; and the fruit thereof shall shake like Lebanon: and they of the city shall flourish like grass of the earth.

His name shall endure for ever: his name shall be continued as long as the sun: and men shall be blessed in him all nations shall call him blessed.

Doxology

Blessed be the LORD God, the God of Israel, who only doeth wondrous things.

And blessed be his glorious name for ever: and let the whole earth be filled with his glory. Amen, and Amen.

A final Postscript

The prayers of David the son of Jesse are ended.

As he dictated that last sentence, it is as if he meant to say, 'If that is how it proves to be for Solomon and for his final Seed, I can ask no more—everything is complete.' And then, exhausted with the effort, he settles back into his pillows. Rather like Simeon in the New Testament who, having seen the infant Jesus brought to him in the temple, said, 'Lord, now lettest thou thy servant depart in peace... for mine eyes have seen thy salvation.' The prayers of Simeon were ended; he had nothing more to ask.

We also would say the same!

We cannot do better than conclude with J. Montgomery's famous hymn, which is a virtual paraphrase of the whole psalm.

Hail to the Lord's Anointed,
Great David's greater Son;
Hail in the time appointed,
His reign on earth begun
He comes to break oppression,
To set the captive free,
To take away transgression,
And rule in equity.

He shall come down like showers,
Upon the fruitful earth;
And love, joy, hope, like flowers,
Spring in His path to birth.
Before Him on the mountains
Shall peace the herald go;
And righteousness in fountains
From hill to valley flow.

Kings shall fall down before Him,
And gold and incense bring,
All nations shall adore Him,
His praise all people sing.
For he shall have dominion
O'er river, sea and shore,
Far as the eagle's pinion
Or dove's light wing can soar.

Amen and Amen!

Appendix 1

David a Type of Christ?

It may seem strange to some to have the Old Testament handled as has been done in this hook, but to ignore the typology and foreshadowings of the Old Testament is to deprive ourselves of one of its most important and exciting values. The Old Testament is full of Christ from the first promise of a coming deliverer in Genesis 3:15, where it is declared that the seed of the woman will bruise the serpent's head, right through to the end of Malachi where 'the Sun of righteousness arises with healing in his wings.' And when He did come, the record of each event and experience He went through is punctuated by the oft-repeated phrase, 'As it is written,' referring back to what is said of Him in the Old Testament.

These foreshadowings of Christ are not only given in direct prophecies, nor only in the types contained in the Mosaic sacrifices and rituals, but also in all sorts of Old Testament personages and incidents. And no Old Testament character is so eminently a type of Christ as David. The old hymn rightly calls Christ 'great David's greater Son'; and in how many points is David a type of that Son! The incidents of his life are redolent with foreshadowings of the gospel, of which Jesus is the centre. It is a preacher's paradise indeed, for it enables him to preach New Testament truths in a vivid pictorial way, and not only in abstract terms; and this pictorial presentation makes the truth more readily assimilated and understood by his hearers.

It may be asked on what Scriptural grounds have we the right to regard David as a type of Christ? I would answer, on the grounds of the messianic psalms, if on no other. There are some of David's psalms where he is in the first place speaking of himself and of his sufferings, but in which you get an uncanny feeling that he is writing bigger than he knows, that he is speaking of Another, and you want to ask what the Ethiopian eunuch asked Philip as he puzzled over Isaiah 53: 'Of whom speaketh the prophet this? of himself, or of some other man?' (Acts 8:34). And then, to your surprise, you find the New Testament taking up some of those very verses and quoting them as either the words of Jesus, or referring directly to Him.

For instance, both Peter and Paul in preaching to the Jews (see Acts 2:25–31; 13:35) picked up the words of Psalm 16, 'Thou wilt not leave my soul in hell, neither wilt thou suffer thine holy one to see corruption,' and made the point that inasmuch as David died and his flesh did see corruption, he must have been speaking, not of himself, but of Another. Peter's interpretation of it was, 'Being a prophet... he spake of the resurrection of Christ, that his soul was not left in hell, neither his flesh did see corruption.' And what shall we say of such psalms as Psalm 22, beginning as it does with the words, 'My God, My God, why hast Thou forsaken Me?', the very words that Jesus uttered on the cross. And as we follow down the psalm we find it contains an exact expression of the feelings of Christ as He died in shame, and of the incidents which took place around that cross. But as far as David was concerned, he doubtless thought that he was only speaking of himself. But we know, in the light of all that happened in the New Testament, that he was speaking of that Other Man, the Messiah, the Lord Jesus.

Other messianic Psalms are: 2, 16, 35, 45, 69, 70, 72, 110, in addition to Psalms 8 and 22 mentioned above. These Scriptures alone give us the warrant to regard David as a foreshadowing of Christ.

Having established that David can be taken as a type of Christ, we then look at his life and adventures and can see in many of the incidents beautiful pictures of the gospel. Then we can go further and see some of the characters surrounding him, some of them unsavoury ones like Saul, as picturing ourselves.

Of course, there are parts of David's life in which he was not at all a foreshadowing of Christ. Typology must not be pressed too far. No Old Testament incident, personage or Mosaic ritual pictures Christ in every particular. Indeed, one of the ways of studying the life of David is to see in it the story of a saint in the making and one who had some grievous falls. Indeed, my friend Dr Alan Redpath has an excellent book on just this aspect of David's life, entitled *The Making of a Man of God*. But my book limits itself to those aspects of his life where he can be taken as a type of Christ, and Saul as a type of ourselves, and where Saul's relationship to David, and David's relationship to Saul, is typical of ours to Him and His to us. Bless His Name that His relationship to us is what it is, in spite of what ours has been to Him!

Appendix 2

Solomon a Type of Christ?

It may be that someone with a questioning mind in reading the last chapter, 'Solomon in All His Glory', may have queried my right to take Solomon so simply as a type of Christ. I think it might be helpful to mention briefly my grounds for doing so.

First of all, Jesus Christ Himself refers to the likeness between Solomon and Himself in the matter of that king's wisdom and glory, only He declares Himself the 'greater than Solomon.'

The words are found in Matthew 12:42—'The queen of the south shall rise up in the judgment with this generation, and shall condemn it: for she came from the uttermost parts of the earth to hear the wisdom of Solomon; and, behold, a greater than Solomon is here.'

More conclusive than this are the words in Hebrews 1:5, where the writer, in seeking to prove the eternal Sonship of Jesus from the Old Testament, quotes the words, 'I will be to him a Father, and he shall be to me a Son.' It is quoted as a clear Old Testament proof text of the divine Sonship of Jesus, and one would imagine it is a direct prophecy concerning Him. What is our surprise on turning to the Old Testament reference concerned (2 Samuel 7:14) to find that God is speaking to David of his heir-to-be, Solomon. It is of Solomon that God says, 'I will be to him a Father, and he shall be to me a son.' And yet in the New Testament the Holy Spirit through the writer to the Hebrews says that it is a reference to Christ. And if the Holy Spirit says so, then for me it is, and it gives me license to look upon Solomon in all his glory as a type of Jesus Christ. If it is permissible to look on David as a foreshadowing of Christ in certain aspects (as I have argued in the previous Appendix), it is also permissible to look on Solomon as a foreshadowing of Christ in other aspects. Of course, as in the case of David, so in that of Solomon—one must not push the type too far. In his later years especially, Solomon was anything but a type or fore-shadowing of Christ.

Then there is this very special Psalm 72 we have been considering. Never was there, to my mind, a clearer case of the Psalmist speaking of one person and going beyond to speak of Another—Jesus Christ. In most messianic psalms it is a case of David speaking firstly of himself and then going beyond to Christ; here it is David speaking of Solomon, and at the same time going beyond to speak of Christ. Whether he thus spoke of Christ wittingly or unwittingly we cannot know. Personally, I believe he knew that he was not only speaking of Solomon, but of Messiah, for he could hardly have claimed for Solomon the universal dominion he speaks of. Rather, 'being a prophet, and knowing that God had sworn with an oath to him, that of the fruit of his loins, according to the flesh, he would raise up Christ to sit on His throne; he seeing this before spake of the resurrection of Christ' (Acts 2:30–31), and not only of the resurrection of Christ, but of the reign of Christ. Certain it is that the church has always looked upon the psalm as messianic. Indeed, two at least of her greatest and best-known hymns have been based upon it: 'Jesus shall reign' and 'Hail to the Lord's Anointed.'

I am aware, of course, that the Revised Standard Version translates the psalm not as consisting of David's prophetic statements concerning Solomon, but rather his prayers for him, and these come out as, 'May he judge thy people with righteousness, and thy poor with justice...' and so on throughout the whole psalm. Presumably the Hebrew could be translated either way, to be decided by the spiritual context of the psalm. To translate it as a prayer is to weaken its messianic character and rob it of much of its glory. One cannot but be sad that the translators of the Revised Standard Version decided to make the sentences prayers rather than prophecies. But not all other revisions have done so; and the saints down the centuries have always with joy hailed the psalm as messianic, and seen in it the glory of the reign of Christ.

RHP Essential Classics

T. AUSTIN-SPARKS
The School of Christ
The inner working of the Holy Spirit

E. M. BOUNDS
Power Through Prayer
A stirring exhortation to pray

JOHN BUNYAN
The Pilgrim's Progress
The classic allegory of the Christian life

CHARLES FINNEY
Revival
God's way of revival

A. P. FITT
D. L. Moody
The life of the great evangelist

ROY HESSION
The Calvary Road
The way of personal revival
Our Nearest Kinsman
The message of hope from the book of Ruth
Not I, but Christ
The Christian's relationship with Jesus explained from the life of David

RHP Essential Classics

ROY HESSION (continued)
The Power of God's Grace
The way of peace, joy and genuine revival
We Would See Jesus
Seeing in Jesus everything we need
When I Saw Him
Renewing your vision of Jesus
My Calvary Road
Roy Hession tells his own story

F. & M. HOWARD TAYLOR
The Biography of James Hudson Taylor
The life of a man of God

DAVID WILKERSON
Hallowed Be Thy Names
Knowing God through His names
Hungry For More of Jesus
The way of intimacy with Christ

ANDREW MURRAY
Absolute Surrender
A call to radical, Spirit-filled Christianity
The Full Blessing of Pentecost
Power from on High
Humility
The way to victory in the Christian life

RHP Essential Classics

ANDREW MURRAY (continued)
The True Vine
Fruitfulness and stability in Jesus
Waiting on God
*Allowing the power of God into our lives and
  ministries*

OSWALD J. SMITH
The Enduement of Power
Being filled with the Holy Spirit
The Man God Uses
How anyone can be used powerfully by God
The Revival We Need
A heart-stirring cry for revival

R. A. TORREY
How to Pray
Praying with power and authority
How to Study the Bible
Profit and pleasure from the Word of God

*Please ask for these titles at your local
Christian bookshop*

RHP Essential Classics

Humility

by Andrew Murray

This book has been definitive in the lives of many. Andrew Murray says that humility lies at the very heart of a successful Christian life. When we came to God for salvation, it was in admitting our need that we found grace. So in every stage of our walk, it is by admitting our lack and realising our utter dependence on God that we are victorious. Moreover, in that God was willing to humble Himself, it is by walking in lowliness of mind that we bear the strongest sign that we are the children of God.

"When I look back upon my own religious experience, or round upon the Church of Christ in the world, I stand amazed at the thought of how little humility is sought after as the distinguishing feature of the discipleship of Jesus. In preaching and living, in the daily intercourse of the home and social life, in the more special fellowship with Christians, in the direction and performance of work for Christ,—alas! how much proof there is that humility is not esteemed the Cardinal virtue, the only route from which the graces can grow, the one indispensable condition of true fellowship with Jesus." —ANDREW MURRAY

ANDREW MURRAY (1828-1917) was born in South Africa where he served God as a pastor and evangelist. His devotional writing brought him world-wide renown and he became much in demand as a Bible teacher and conference speaker. Author of numerous books, his other titles include *The True Vine*, *Absolute Surrender*, *The Full Blessing of Pentecost* and *Waiting on God*.

RHP Essential Classics

The Man God Uses
by Oswald J. Smith

This is an incredibly powerful book which gets to the heart of the Christian life. It contains both foundational teaching about victorious living but also very insightful instruction about authentic Christianity, and how one's whole life can be used in effective service for God. Few other writers can speak as incisively as Oswald J. Smith; although written several generations ago, this is essential reading for our day.

"You want God to use you? Well, then, are you willing to pay the price? Are you prepared to let everything else go and become a man of one thing? Will you devote your entire life to this one thing, to see to it that nothing else attracts you, that nothing else interests you, nothing else absorbs your attention? Are you prepared to concentrate, to give yourself wholly to God's service, to become a man of one great purpose in life? If you are, God will use you for His glory and honour, and your evangelism will be successful."

—OSWALD J. SMITH

"His books have been used by the Holy Spirit to sear into the very depths of my own soul and have had a tremendous influence on my personal life and ministry."

— BILLY GRAHAM

RHP Essential Classics

Power Through Prayer
by E. M. Bounds

E. M. Bounds has a message: We need to pray. Whereas much of the church is focussing on methods and education, Bounds says the answer to the lack of power in Christian service is simply prayer. Bounds identifies the errors that many make which lead to failure, and uses the lives of great men of God as examples to show the absolute necessity of a serious prayer life. This rousing exhortation should leave a deep impression.

"What the Church needs today is not more machinery or better, not new organizations or more and novel methods, but men whom the Holy Spirit can use—men of prayer, men mighty in prayer. The Holy Spirit does not flow through methods, but through men. He does not come on machinery, but on men. He does not anoint plans, but men—men of prayer."

—E. M. BOUNDS

EDWARD MCKENDREE BOUNDS studied law and went on to practise as an attorney for several years. During the Third Great Awakening in America, he felt the call to preach. At the age of twenty-four he was made Pastor of Missouri Methodist Church. He pastored several successful churches, but was above all known as a man of prayer, rising to pray for three hours each morning. His writings on prayer have been best-sellers ever since.

RHP Essential Classics

Absolute Surrender
by Andrew Murray

This is a very important book. In it, Andrew Murray gives comprehensive teaching on key aspects of living a deeper Christian life—a life that counts for something: how to be filled with the Spirit and how to walk in the Spirit; the conditions for fruitful service; the need for absolute surrender; how to walk in victory. This book gives an essential grounding for those who wish to take the Christian life seriously and to be used greatly in the things of God.

"When God clothes the lily with its beauty, is it not yielded up, surrendered, given over to God as He works in it its beauty? And God's redeemed children, oh, can you think that God can work His work if there is only half or a part of them surrendered? God cannot do it. God is life, and love, and blessing, and power, and infinite beauty, and God delights to communicate Himself to every child who is prepared to receive Him; but ah! this one want of absolute surrender is just the thing that hinders God. And now He comes, and as God He claims it."

—ANDREW MURRAY

ANDREW MURRAY (1828-1917) was born in South Africa where he served God as a pastor and evangelist. His devotional writing brought him world-wide renown and he became much in demand as a Bible teacher and conference speaker. Author of numerous books, his other titles include *The True Vine*, *Humility*, *The Full Blessing of Pentecost* and *Waiting on God*.

RHP Essential Classics

The School of Christ
by T. Austin-Sparks

Introduction by DAVID WILKERSON

"Are you moving on in the growing fulness of the revelation of the Lord Jesus? Have you an open heaven? Is God in Christ revealing Himself to you in ever greater wonder and fullness?

The ministry contained in this little book has been wrought on the anvil of deep and drastic dealings of God with the vessel. It is not only doctrinal: it is experiential. Only those who really mean business with God will take the pains demanded to read it.

Of all the books that have issued from this ministry, I regard this one as that which goes most deeply to the roots and foundations of our life in Christ with God.

May He make the reading of it result in a fuller understanding of the meaning of Christ."

—T. AUSTIN-SPARKS

"This is a book you will want to read many times. It was during my third reading that its truth fully dawned on me. It has affected my preaching, my outlook on life, and intensified my hunger for the glorious liberty of the Cross. We believe this book is destined by God to bless and edify numerous spiritually hungry ministers and laymen."

—DAVID WILKERSON

RHP Essential Classics

Waiting on God
by Andrew Murray

The importance of waiting on God cannot be over-emphasized. In a world marked by frenetic activity, Andrew Murray shows that this unspectacular work opens the door to God's power in any situation. When our instinct calls us to work, it is often more important to wait—that is, to look to God to come into the situation—and then to work in His power.

"All that the Church and its members need for the manifestation of the mighty power of God in the world is the return to our true place, the place of absolute and unceasing dependence upon God. Let us strive to see what the elements are that make up this most blessed and needful waiting upon God. It may help us to discover the reasons why this grace is so little cultivated, and to feel how infinitely desirable it is that the Church, that we ourselves, should at any price learn its blessed secret."

—ANDREW MURRAY

ANDREW MURRAY (1828-1917) was born in South Africa where he served God as a pastor and evangelist. His devotional writing brought him world-wide renown and he became much in demand as a Bible teacher and conference speaker. Author of numerous books, his other titles include *The True Vine*, *Humility*, *The Full Blessing of Pentecost* and *Waiting on God*.

RHP Essential Classics

The Life of D. L. Moody
by A. P. Fitt

D. L. Moody had a profound effect not just on his native America but on Great Britain and other countries as well, and his name continues to be known across the world as one of the great men of God through history. But what shaped the man? How did he get to the place where he was so mightily used by God? How did he live? What were his methods of working? For those wanting to learn some of the secrets of effective ministry, much can be gleaned from reading this account of his life. Written by his son-in-law, it makes for gripping reading.

"Moody once heard someone say 'The world has yet to see what God can do with, and for, and through, and in a man who is fully and wholly consecrated to Him.' The statement took hold of him. He thought to himself, 'I will try my utmost to be that man.'

"The hunger for more spiritual power was upon him. 'I was crying all the time that God would fill me with His Spirit. Well, one day, in the city of New York—ah, what a day!—I cannot describe it, I seldom refer to it; it is almost too sacred an experience to name. I can only say God revealed Himself to me, and I had such an experience of His love that I had to ask Him to stay His hand. I went to preaching again. The sermons were not different; I did not present any new truths; and yet hundreds were converted.'"

—A. P. FITT